New Directions for
Teaching and Learning

Marilla D. Svinicki
EDITOR-IN-CHIEF

R. Eugene Rice
CONSULTING EDITOR

Self-Authorship:
Advancing Students'
Intellectual Growth

Peggy S. Meszaros
EDITOR

Number 109 • Spring 2007
Jossey-Bass
San Francisco

SELF-AUTHORSHIP: ADVANCING STUDENTS' INTELLECTUAL GROWTH
Peggy S. Meszaros (ed.)
New Directions for Teaching and Learning, no. 109
Marilla D. Svinicki, Editor-in-Chief
R. *Eugene Rice*, Consulting Editor

Microfilm copies of issues and articles are available in 16mm and 35mm, as well as microfiche in 105mm, through University Microfilms, Inc., 300 North Zeeb Road, Ann Arbor, Michigan 48106-1346.

NEW DIRECTIONS FOR TEACHING AND LEARNING (ISSN 0271-0633, electronic ISSN 1536-0768) is part of The Jossey-Bass Higher and Adult Education Series and is published quarterly by Wiley Subscription Services, Inc., A Wiley Company, at Jossey-Bass, 989 Market Street, San Francisco, California 94103-1741. Periodicals postage paid at San Francisco, California, and at additional mailing offices. POSTMASTER: Send address changes to New Directions for Teaching and Learning, Jossey-Bass, 989 Market Street, San Francisco, California 94103-1741.

New Directions for Teaching and Learning is indexed in College Student Personnel Abstracts, Contents Pages in Education, and Current Index to Journals in Education (ERIC).

SUBSCRIPTIONS cost $80 for individuals and $195 for institutions, agencies, and libraries in the United States. Prices subject to change. See order form at end of book.

EDITORIAL CORRESPONDENCE should be sent to the editor-in-chief, Marilla D. Svinicki, Department of Educational Psychology, University of Texas at Austin, One University Station, D5800, Austin, TX 78712.

www.josseybass.com

CONTENTS

BICENTENNIAL
1807
⊛WILEY
2007
BICENTENNIAL
BICENTENNIAL
BICENTENNIAL

The Wiley Bicentennial—Knowledge for Generations

*E*ach generation has its unique needs and aspirations. When Charles Wiley first opened his small printing shop in lower Manhattan in 1807, it was a generation of boundless potential searching for an identity. And we were there, helping to define a new American literary tradition. Over half a century later, in the midst of the Second Industrial Revolution, it was a generation focused on building the future. Once again, we were there, supplying the critical scientific, technical, and engineering knowledge that helped frame the world. Throughout the 20th Century, and into the new millennium, nations began to reach out beyond their own borders and a new international community was born. Wiley was there, expanding its operations around the world to enable a global exchange of ideas, opinions, and know-how.

For 200 years, Wiley has been an integral part of each generation's journey, enabling the flow of information and understanding necessary to meet their needs and fulfill their aspirations. Today, bold new technologies are changing the way we live and learn. Wiley will be there, providing you the must-have knowledge you need to imagine new worlds, new possibilities, and new opportunities.

Generations come and go, but you can always count on Wiley to provide you the knowledge you need, when and where you need it!

WILLIAM J. PESCE
PRESIDENT AND CHIEF EXECUTIVE OFFICER

PETER BOOTH WILEY
CHAIRMAN OF THE BOARD

FROM THE SERIES EDITOR

About This Publication. Since 1980, *New Directions for Teaching and Learning (NDTL)* has brought a unique blend of theory, research, and practice to leaders in postsecondary education. *NDTL* sourcebooks strive not only for solid substance but also for timeliness, compactness, and accessibility.

The series has four goals: to inform readers about current and future directions in teaching and learning in postsecondary education, to illuminate the context that shapes these new directions, to illustrate these new directions through examples from real settings, and to propose ways in which these new directions can be incorporated into still other settings.

This publication reflects the view that teaching deserves respect as a high form of scholarship. We believe that significant scholarship is conducted not only by researchers who report results of empirical investigations but also by practitioners who share disciplined reflections about teaching. Contributors to *NDTL* approach questions of teaching and learning as seriously as they approach substantive questions in their own disciplines, and they deal not only with pedagogical issues but also with the intellectual and social context in which these issues arise. Authors deal on the one hand with theory and research and on the other with practice, and they translate from research and theory to practice and back again.

About This Volume. The goal of education should be to help students develop as self-reflective, self-aware individuals, but the practice has not always matched the promise. The chapters in this issue offer some ways to help students on their journey of self-discovery and growth.

Marilla D. Svinicki
Editor-in-Chief

MARILLA D. SVINICKI is associate professor of educational psychology at the University of Texas at Austin.

EDITOR'S NOTES

The genesis of the idea for this volume began as I served as the senior vice president and provost of Virginia Tech through the 1990s. I had been pondering questions about student intellectual growth over the past twenty years as I held various administrative roles in universities. Each of these institutions had major or minor plans to focus on the education of the whole person, and some actually had identified what a college education was all about by determining general student learning outcomes. But measurement of these outcomes was always a major stumbling block, and so the plans went on a shelf to be produced when the next crisis came from the higher education oversight committee, an accrediting agency, or some legislator demanding greater accountability from the institution.

The seriousness of seeking answers for the intellectual growth of students hit when I realized that as provost, I had responsibility for a major academic enterprise with thousands of undergraduate and graduate students, their academic programs, and their progress toward degrees. This reality brought the focus of my attention in 1993 back to student learning outcomes. At the same time, public cries for accountability from higher education were again building in state legislatures around the country, including in Virginia. Our response had been to require academic departments to produce five-year plans displaying their students' progress from recruitment to graduation and professional careers. A review of most of those plans revealed perfunctory responses to superficial and simplistic questions, with little attention given to identifying and measuring intellectual growth. The intellectual growth of students was clearly not a central focus for academic work but rather was attended to when a report was called for and produced to verify the task was done.

Given that faculty are usually prepared only in their subject matter, with little knowledge or experience with theoretical or pedagogical frameworks for understanding learning in its broadest sense, it is not hard to see why progress has been slow in obtaining consensus on student learning outcomes or measurement issues. What seems to be missing for most institutions and most faculties is a theoretical framework for understanding what is happening as learning takes place and the supports needed to advance this learning. This volume seeks to fill this void with one theoretical framework and examples of its use in student engagement and discovery.

I was introduced to the theory of self-authorship (Baxter Magolda, 2001) when I returned to my faculty role in 2001 and worked with colleagues to

NEW DIRECTIONS FOR TEACHING AND LEARNING, no. 109, Spring 2007 © Wiley Periodicals, Inc.
Published online in Wiley InterScience (www.interscience.wiley.com) • DOI: 10.1002/tl.260

1

produce a research grant funded by the National Science Foundation exploring how girls make information technology career decisions using the theoretical framework of self-authorship. This framework was ideal to foster understanding of a student's ways of making meaning of complex decisions, including career decisions.

This volume is a direct result of further collaborations with colleagues as applications of the theory have resulted in development of assessment measures, innovative curricular programs, and research to answer important student learning outcome questions. A symposium presentation at the American Education Research Association in 2005 brought the chapter authors together, and the idea of sharing our findings with a larger audience was born.

A major contribution of this volume is to expose college faculty, student personnel faculty and staff, and college administrators to the theoretical framework of self-authorship and its link to addressing student learning outcomes. The illustrations of the intellectual development of students as they make their journey toward self-authorship with multiple examples of the Learning Partnerships Model (LPM) provide real-life stories to guide educational practice. First identified by Kegan (1994) and further developed by Baxter Magolda (2001), the promise of this framework is explained in Chapter One as the LPM is described alongside an overview of the literature documenting current attempts to identify student learning outcomes in higher education. Chapter Two provides new benchmarks for student learning outcomes and identifies the challenges that higher education institutions face when they embrace changing old paradigms for teaching, learning, and measurement of outcomes. The authors of Chapters Three, Four, and Five explore applications of self-authorship and describe the development and use of assessment instruments and applications for research and curriculum development. Chapter Six sums up the promise of self-authorship and challenges readers to reenvision their educational practice, and Chapter Seven suggests next steps on the journey to using self-authorship as a framework for substantial change and improvement.

The audiences for this volume are broad, ranging from college faculty to student affairs faculty and staff and college administrators facing assessment challenges for reporting student learning outcomes to their various constituencies, agencies, and boards. This volume should also prove instructive to faculty embarking on curriculum revisions and identifying and measuring student learning outcomes for undergraduate and graduate students.

Challenge and support are key concepts in producing self-authored young people. Throughout this volume, the challenge of producing work that will influence substantial educational practice change is evident. The support the chapter authors offered one another through the production of this volume and our ongoing efforts of collaboration sustain our passion and belief in this framework. We hope that this volume will not only be read but also will be used as a guide as learning outcomes are structured and educational practice is envisioned that will truly advance the intellectual growth of all students everywhere.

Peggy S. Meszaros
Editor

References

Baxter Magolda, M. B. *Making Their Own Way: Narratives for Transforming Higher Education to Promote Self-Development.* Sterling, Va.: Stylus, 2001.
Kegan, R. *In over Our Heads: The Mental Demands of Modern Life.* Cambridge, Mass.: Harvard University Press, 1994.

PEGGY S. MESZAROS is the William E. Lavery Professor of Human Development and director of the Center for Information Technology Impacts on Children, Youth, and Families at Virginia Polytechnic Institute and State University in Blacksburg, Virginia.

1

This chapter presents the need for the journey of self-authorship and an overview of key concepts and terms explored in this volume.

The Journey of Self-Authorship: Why Is It Necessary?

Peggy S. Meszaros

> Education is what survives when what has been learnt has been forgotten.
>
> B. F. Skinner

Nowhere today are the increasing public cries for accountability in higher education heard louder than in student learning outcomes. The expectations of higher education in the twenty-first century include overarching goals of effective citizenship and outcomes such as critical thinking, mature decision making, appreciation of multiple perspectives and difference, and interdependent relationships with others (Baxter Magolda, 2004a). These broad goals go considerably beyond mere knowledge of subject matter and require a new lens to view learning and teaching in higher education.

An understanding of developmental transformations and a theoretical framework are required if broader learning expectations are to be met. The theoretical framework of self-authorship, as identified by Kegan (1994) and Baxter Magolda (1992, 1999), offers a context for examining these transformations and developing effective responses to students' intellectual growth through the lens of self-authorship. The Learning Partnerships Model (LPM) (Baxter Magolda, 2004b) that grows from the tenets of self-authorship provides a practice model linking learning and development for implementing the transformations that students need to become self-authored. This

NEW DIRECTIONS FOR TEACHING AND LEARNING, no. 109, Spring 2007 © Wiley Periodicals, Inc.
Published online in Wiley InterScience (www.interscience.wiley.com) • DOI: 10.1002/tl.261

volume presents the urgent case for professional and institutional transformation and examples of using the lens of self-authorship as a framework for educators to consider as courses are structured, research designed, and outreach developed and implemented.

The necessity and urgency for a new look at how we prepare college students will be evident in this chapter's synopsis of recent national reports and discussions about the preparation of college students. These efforts to measure and report student learning in higher education seem headed for narrow national testing of subject matter knowledge without consideration of the broader goals of a college education and a self-authored citizen. What is missing in all the calls for more accountability for students' intellectual growth is an understanding of a theoretical context for developmental transformations and a model for implementing the teaching and learning process that fosters growth. The goal of this volume is to fill the void for this understanding. This chapter explains terms and concepts used throughout the volume and introduces the LPM, a holistic practice model that brings together within a common framework the theory of self-authorship, development, and instruction.

Other chapters in this volume provide examples of how to assess self-authorship, how to use the theory in research to understand how students make self-authored decisions, and how to develop innovative curricula using the lens of self-authorship and the LPM. A chapter on needed institutional changes if we are to take student learning seriously and a chapter summarizing the promise of self-authorship with further case examples of the LPM provide ideas for transforming educational practice. Finally, a chapter of next steps with suggestions for advancing the journey of self-authorship completes the volume.

The urgency and necessity for educators to embrace the journey of self-authorship and the LPM for improving college student learning outcomes become clearer as we view national efforts currently underway to shape the dialogue in narrower ways.

National Efforts to Improve Student Learning

Higher education institutions in the United States have kept pace with and have often led the rest of the world in providing students with powerful new technologies, new dynamics of communication, and new connections to faculty as knowledge has been created. However, serious learning issues are now surfacing, and the call to improve college student learning is being revisited by organizations such as the Business-Higher Education Forum (2003, 2004), the Council for Higher Education Accreditation (2003), the State Higher Education Executive Officers (2005), the Association of American Colleges and Universities (2004; Schneider and Miller, 2005), and the National Center for Public Policy and Higher Education (2005; Miller and Ewell, 2005). It is apparent from each of these major reports that student learning outcomes are rapidly taking center stage as the principal gauge of the effectiveness of higher education.

As further evidence of the growing concern of fostering the intellectual development of college students, three major efforts are under way to shape the national discussion of preparing higher education students to compete in the new global economy. The first of these efforts involves accreditation of academic programs and institutions. In September 2003 the Council for Higher Education Accreditation produced its *Statement of Mutual Responsibilities for Student Learning Outcomes: Accreditation, Institutions, and Programs*. This statement identified a common responsibility for institutions and accrediting agencies in policing themselves and preparing for external review. This common expectation focuses on student learning outcomes and calls for institutions to regularly gather and report concrete evidence about what students know and can do as a result of their respective courses of study. This evidence must be framed in terms of established learning outcomes and supplied at an appropriate level of aggregation. The document amplifies this expectation of mutual responsibilities by providing an indepth background statement on accreditation and student learning. A clear need is cited for accrediting organizations to augment the information reported about student learning resources and processes with more easily understood information about what students know and can do as a consequence of their attending various institutions and programs. It was anticipated that this call for direct measures of student learning and ease of public understanding would be echoed in the report of the federal Commission on the Future of Higher Education issued in September 2006.

On September 19, 2005, U.S. Secretary of Education Margaret Spellings announced the formation of the Secretary of Education's Commission on the Future of Higher Education (Babyak and Glickman, 2005). The new commission was charged with developing a comprehensive national strategy for postsecondary education that will meet the needs of America's diverse population while also addressing the economic and workforce needs of the country's future. A nineteen–member commission appointed by Secretary Spellings is composed of representatives from business, educational organizations, and institutions, with Charles Miller, an outspoken critic of education from Texas, as chair. Miller has been an architect of change in the Texas education system for over two decades and helped create two major accountability systems in the state: the accountability system for public schools that became the model for the No Child Left Behind Act and a method of accountability testing for the University of Texas System. Although all commission members will weigh in on the final report, a heavy reliance on accountability testing in higher education was a logical expectation given Miller's urging to test college students as a way of measuring what they have learned. In anticipation of the commission's report, the national conversation was broadened through discussion among college and university presidents and provosts in summer 2006.

The National Association of State Universities and Land Grant Colleges (NASULGC) prepared a discussion paper released in April 2006, "Improving Student Learning in Higher Education Through Better Accountability and Assessment," coauthored by Peter McPherson, president of NASULGC, and David Shulenburger, vice president of academic affairs. This paper was discussed by university presidents and provosts representing nearly all four-year public colleges and universities in the United States at their 2006 summer meetings and recommendations were shared with the Spellings Commission staff. In laying out the many attempts over the past few decades to better understand the complexities and outcomes of higher education, the authors conclude that no single system accurately reflects and compares the critical facts easily understood by all interested parties, serves as an effective instrument for continuous quality improvement, and is flexible and dynamic. Emphasizing that the very diversity of our U.S. decentralized organization of higher education is its greatest strength, the paper urges consideration of a voluntary system by type or mission of colleges and universities and one that is based on outcomes. Restating a deep commitment to improving student learning, McPherson and Shulenburger call for a serious discussion within the higher education community on how best to improve current efforts and consider a voluntary system to improve student learning.

These three recent developments will keep alive the conversations about student learning with an emphasis on measuring direct outcomes of learning and reporting to the public in easily understood terms. The fact that all three efforts are currently under way and outcomes of their deliberations likely focus solely on knowledge attainment, with a national testing program of skills probably resulting, is troubling if we believe a more holistic picture of student learning is necessary. These developments make clear the need to consider seriously the journey of self-authorship as a viable model for improving the transformations necessary for college students to meet higher education's overarching goals. This volume responds to the call from NASULGC for serious discussion within the higher education community on how best to improve our current efforts and consider a voluntary system to improve student learning. Before proceeding with chapters that explain and give examples of the theory framework and the LPM practice model, we need a common understanding of concepts and definitions that appear throughout this volume.

Definitions

Three key terms are threaded throughout this volume: *student intellectual development, student learning outcomes,* and *self-authorship.*

Student Intellectual Development. Student intellectual development at the postsecondary level has become a global concern as agencies, institutions, and governments struggle to identify what is essential for college students to learn to function fully in the twenty-first century and how to measure these learning outcomes. Indexes of student learning that are both credible and easily understood by the public are necessary and currently missing. Theories of student learning, particularly higher-order learning, are important in helping us understand the student intellectual development that underpins student learning. Discussions of a theory base are noticeably missing in the national conversations; nevertheless, they must underpin our holistic view of college student development.

Although there are different orientations to understanding student intellectual development through various theoretical lenses, the research begun by Perry (1968) and extended by Baxter Magolda (1992) undergirds the chapters in this volume and helps us understand the metaphor of a journey that students undertake as they move through their college years. Perry's work on the stages of intellectual development identified nine stages of this journey that college students move through with respect to intellectual development. The nine positions can be grouped into four categories: (1) dualism/received knowledge, where authorities have the knowledge and students must learn the answers; (2) multiplicity/subjective knowledge, where there are conflicting answers, and students must trust their inner voices, not the external authority; (3) relativism/procedural knowledge, where there are disciplinary reasoning methods; and (4) commitment/constructed knowledge, where students integrate the knowledge they learn from others with their own personal experience and reflection. This journey through the stages can be repeated, and a student may be at different stages at the same time with respect to different subjects.

Perry's interviews were conducted with a small sample of primarily male students at a medium-sized private university almost four decades ago. More recently, Marcia Baxter Magolda's work builds on Perry's research using the journey metaphor and changes in students' construction of meaning or ways of knowing from absolute knowing, through transitional and independent knowing, to contextual knowing. Her longitudinal research began with a study in 1986 with 101 first-year college students. Her goal was to better understand learning and intellectual development during college. Although these initial interviews were helpful in understanding different ways of knowing during college, Baxter Magolda (2001) recognized the need to continue her study to a postcollege phase and expand her investigation of intellectual development to include how participants viewed themselves and their interconnections with others. Perhaps the best way to understand the broader definition of student intellectual development used in this volume is through her own words:

> College educators share a common goal—to guide college students through this transformation to develop mature ways of making informed judgments. Moving away from uncritical acceptance of knowledge to critically constructing one's own perspective, however, is more complex than learning a skill set. It is a transformation of how we think—a change in our assumptions about the certainty, source and limits of knowledge. The evolution of assumptions about knowledge from certain and possessed by authorities to context dependent

judgment based on relevant evidence is what researchers call intellectual or epistemological development [Baxter Magolda, 2006, p. 50].

Student Learning Outcomes. Agreement on common learning goals and outcomes for college students, and therefore what is measured, sounds deceptively simple. In fact, achieving agreement is complex given the diversity of higher education institutions, their missions, and their visions, leading often to narrow, easy-to-measure outcomes. In a poll conducted by the National Center for Public Policy and Higher Education, the public indicated that the following broad goals were "absolutely essential" for higher education (Shavelson and Huang, 2003):

- Sense of maturity and ability to manage on one's own—71 percent
- Ability to get along with people different from one's self—68 percent
- Problem-solving and thinking ability—63 percent
- High-technology skills—61 percent
- Specific expertise and knowledge in a chosen career—60 percent
- Top-notch writing and speaking ability—57 percent
- Responsibilities of citizenship—44 percent

Many others weigh in on the definition of student learning outcomes. Most recently, Derek Bok (2006) in his book *Our Underachieving Colleges* cites several purposes he believes go beyond intellectual development and are essential for all college graduates: learning to communicate, learning to think, building character, preparing for citizenship, living with diversity, preparing for a global society, acquiring broader interests, and preparing for a career.

While it is up to each institution to define the learning goals and outcomes for its students, the definition I use is related to the journey of self-authorship and the ends we seek in the journey that college provides. Again, the words of Baxter Magolda provide the definition used in this volume:

> Educators have multiple expectations for the journey that is called a college education. For example, we expect students to acquire knowledge, learn how to analyze it, and learn the process of judging what to believe themselves— what developmental theorists call complex ways of knowing. We expect students to develop an internal sense of identity—an understanding of how they view themselves and what they value. We expect them to learn how to construct healthy relationships with others, relationships based on mutuality rather than self-sacrifice, and relationships that affirm diversity. We expect them to integrate these ways of knowing, being and interacting with others into the capacity for self-authorship—the capacity to internally define their own beliefs, identity, and relationships. This self-authorship, this internal capacity, is the necessary foundation for mutual, collaborative participation with others in adult life [Baxter Magolda, 2001, p. xvi].

Self-Authorship. The words of one of Baxter Magolda's students, Mark, build on the definition of self-authorship in the preceding paragraph as he struggles to define his own beliefs, identity, and relationships: "Making yourself into something, not what other people say or not just kind of floating along in life, but you're in some sense a piece of clay. You've been formed into different things, but that doesn't mean you can't go back on the potter's wheel and instead of somebody else's hands building and molding you, you use your own, and in a fundamental sense change your values and beliefs."

Mark clearly articulated the move into self-authorship he and his peers made in their mid- to late twenties. During this time, the tide turned in the clash between internal voice and external influence. Participants' internal voices grew strong enough to supersede external influence, and although external influence remained a part of their lives, it was now relegated to the background as the internal voice took the foreground. The internal voice, or self, became the coordinator and mediator of external influence. As Mark said, participants began to use their own hands to build and mold themselves and their beliefs.

Becoming the authors of their own lives involved reshaping what they believed (epistemology), their sense of self (intrapersonal), and their relationships with others (interpersonal). Participants shifted from "how you know" to "how I know" and in doing so began to choose their own beliefs. They acknowledged the inherent uncertainty of knowledge and took up the challenge of choosing what to believe in this context. They also attempted to live out their beliefs in their work and personal lives. At the same time, "how I know" required determining who the "I" was. Intense self-reflection and interaction with others helped participants gain perspective on themselves and begin to choose their own values and identity. This emerging sense of self required renegotiation of existing relationships that had been built on external approval at the expense of personal needs and the creation of new mutual relationships consistent with the internal voice (Baxter Magolda, 2001). This explanation of self-authorship prepares us to take a look at the practice model that grows from this understanding and provides a road map for the journey and the transitions along the way.

Learning Partnerships Model

The transitions required for the journey of self-authorship take time, energy, and guidance from a variety of dedicated educators. This complex journey ideally begins for students at the outset of college. For the journey to be successful, faculty and student development professionals must place self-authorship as the central goal of higher education and provide a new form of guidance for teaching and learning. This new form of guidance, the LPM, emphasizes challenge and support and brings together two traditionally separate worlds in academe: cognition and affect. Students experience the classroom, or curricular, with its emphasis on knowledge, and they concurrently experience student life, or the cocurricular, with its emphasis on affect. Too often these two worlds do not meet or coordinate despite an avowed preference found in the college recruitment literature for education of the whole person. The LPM provides a bridge or pattern for collaboration between the two worlds.

The chapters that follow provide an in-depth look at understanding the LPM, the self-authorship theory behind it, and multiple examples of its application. It is important to have a good understanding of the model, and I offer a simple metaphor to help in visualizing it. To fully understand the LPM, think about a journey you may be planning. You will need some form of transportation, a road map with signs along the way to guide your journey, and a final destination. Now visualize your transportation as a tandem bicycle. There is a rider on the front, the student, who decides the direction and is in charge of making decisions. The rider on the back is you, the teacher or student affairs professional, who stokes the bike, providing challenge and support for the student on the front. You provide the elements of challenge and support in your teaching and mentoring (you might picture them as the saddlebags for the journey). Keeping challenge and support in balance as the student heads in the direction of self-authorship is part of your role and a key element of the model. The guideposts are found as students move from absolute knowing, the first marker; through transitional or independent knowing, the second marker; to contextual knowing, the final destination. This visual and simple depiction of the LPM is a metaphor for an in-depth understanding of the model that appears in the following chapters but helps us see the ideal of the partnership, as the student and the educator are good company for each other on the journey. For a deeper understanding of the model we turn again to the words of Baxter Magolda (2004c):

> Learning partnerships support self-authorship via three principles: validating learners' capacity as knowledge constructors, situating learning in learners' experience, and defining learning as mutually constructing meaning. Validating learners' capacity to learn and construct knowledge is necessary for them to realize that they can go back to the potter's wheel. Situating learning in their experience instead of the experience of authority gives them a context from which to bring their identity to learning. Defining learning as a mutual process of exchanging perspectives to arrive at knowledge claims supports their participation in the social construction of knowledge. The three principles model autonomy through encouraging learners to bring their experience and construct their own perspectives. The principles model connection through encouraging learners to connect to their own and others' experience and ideas [pp. xix, xx].

A Necessary New Lens for the Journey

As national calls for a new emphasis on student learning outcomes take center stage and become the principal gauge of higher education's effectiveness, faculty and administrators need a broader, more holistic framework for understanding and fostering student intellectual growth. The conceptual framework for this volume, which addresses the need for a new lens to understand student intellectual growth and responds to the call from NASULGC for serious discussion within the higher education community on how best to improve our efforts, provides an innovative perspective that is gained from the theory of self-authorship and the LPM. Practical examples of the use of this new lens fill the chapters that follow and conclude with a chapter to spark involvement in the next steps on this journey of student intellectual transformations.

References

Association of American Colleges and Universities. *Our Students' Best Work: A Framework for Accountability Worthy of Our Mission.* Washington, D.C.: Association of American Colleges and Universities, 2004. Retrieved May 10, 2006, from http://www.aacu_edu.org/About/Statements/assessment.cfm.

Babyak, S., and Glickman, J. "Secretary Spellings Announces New Commission on the Future of Higher Education." Press release, Sept. 19, 2005. Retrieved May 16, 2006, from http: www.ed.gov/pressreleases/2005/09/09192995.html.

Baxter Magolda, M. B. *Knowing and Reasoning in College: Gender-Related Patterns in Students' Intellectual Development.* San Francisco: Jossey-Bass, 1992.

Baxter Magolda, M. B. *Creating Contexts for Learning and Self-Authorship.* Nashville, Tenn.: Vanderbilt University Press, 1999.

Baxter Magolda, M. B. *Making Their Own Way: Narratives for Transforming Higher Education to Promote Self-Development.* Sterling, Va.: Stylus, 2001.

Baxter Magolda, M. B. "Self-Authorship as the Common Goal of 21st Century Education." In M. B. Baxter Magolda and P. M. King (eds.), *Learning Partnerships: Theory and Models of Practice to Educate for Self-Authorship.* Sterling, Va.: Stylus, 2004a.

Baxter Magolda, M. B. "Learning Partnerships Model: A Framework for Promoting Self-Authorship." In M. B. Baxter Magolda and P. M. King (eds.), *Learning Partnerships: Theory and Models of Practice to Educate for Self-Authorship.* Sterling, Va.: Stylus, 2004b.

Baxter Magolda, M. B. "Preface." In M. B. Baxter Magolda and P. M. King (eds.), *Learning Partnerships: Theory and Models of Practice to Educate for Self-Authorship.* Sterling, Va.: Stylus, 2004c.

Baxter Magolda, M. B. "Intellectual Development in the College Years." *Change,* 2006, 38(3), 50–54.

Bok, D. *Our Underachieving Colleges.* Princeton, N.J.: Princeton University Press, 2006.

Business-Higher Education Forum. *Building a Nation of Learners: The Need for Changes in Teaching and Learning to Meet Global Challenges.* Washington, D.C.: Business-Higher Education Forum, 2003. Retrieved May 1, 2006, from http://www.bhef.com/publications/.

Business-Higher Education Forum. *Public Accountability for Student Learning in Higher Education: Issues and Options.* Washington, D.C.: Business-Higher Education Forum, 2004. Retrieved May 1, 2006, from http://www.bhef.com/publications/.

Council for Higher Education Accreditation. *Statement of Mutual Responsibilities for Student Learning Outcomes: Accreditation, Institutions, and Programs.* Washington, D.C.: Council for Higher Education Accreditation, 2003. Retrieved Apr. 25, 2006, from http://www.chea.org/Research/index.asp#statements.

Kegan, R. *In over Our Heads: The Mental Demands of Modern Life.* Cambridge, Mass.: Harvard University Press, 1994.

McPherson, P., and Shulenburger, D. "Improving Student Learning in Higher Education Through Better Accountability and Assessment." Discussion paper, National Association of State Universities and Land-Grant Colleges, 2006.

Miller, M. A., and Ewell, P. T. *Measuring Up on College-Level Learning.* Washington, D.C.: National Center for Public Policy and Higher Education, Oct. 2005. Retrieved May 10, 2006, from http://www.highereducation.org/reports/mu_learning/index.shtml.

National Center for Public Policy and Higher Education. *Income of U.S. Workers Projected to Decline If Education Doesn't Improve.* Washington, D.C.: National Center for Public Policy and Higher Education, Nov. 9, 2005. Retrieved May 10, 2006, from http://www.highereducation.org/reports/pa_decline/index.shtml.

Perry, W. P. *Forms of Intellectual and Ethical Development in the College Years: A Scheme.* Austin, Tex.: Holt, 1968.

Schneider, C. G., and Miller, R. *Liberal Education Outcomes: A Preliminary Report on Student Achievement in College.* Washington, D.C.: Association of American Colleges and Universities, 2005. Retrieved May 10, 2006, from http://www.highereducation.org/reports/mu_learning/Learning.pdf.

Shavelson, R. J., and Huang, L. "Responding Responsibly to the Frenzy to Assess Learning in Higher Education." *Change,* Jan.–Feb. 2003, pp. 10–19. Retrieved Apr. 13, 2006, from http://www.standford.edu/dept/SUSE/SEAL.

State Higher Education Executive Officers. *Report of the National Commission on Accountability in Higher Education.* Boulder, Colo.: State Higher Education Executive Officers, Mar. 10, 2005. Retrieved May 10, 2006, from http://www.Sheeo.org/pubs/pubs_search.asp.

PEGGY S. MESZAROS is the William E. Lavery Professor of Human Development and director of the Center for Information Technology Impacts on Children, Youth, and Families at Virginia Polytechnic Institute and State University in Blacksburg, Virginia.

2

Student learning and student development are part of a unified framework rather than separate interests to be pursued independently.

Taking Seriously the Intellectual Growth of Students: Accommodations for Self-Authorship

Terry M. Wildman

Self-authorship is proposed as a developmental goal fundamental to successful adaptation in the world of the twenty-first century (Baxter Magolda, 2004). Cast in educational terms, the basic premise is that schools serve not only to keep and convey knowledge, but also to provide those special assistive conditions that can nudge minds to life. This assertion of new roles for schools is a natural progression of the growing body of research showing how education can shape development, but also how epistemological development is essential for effective learning. As this reciprocal relationship—this more complex story line about student learning—becomes increasingly clarified, schools will face increasing pressure to respond. We now know with much greater clarity that sound education requires bringing the student along for the journey. The argument for taking intellectual development seriously can be thought of as protecting the massive investment already being made in traditional approaches to education.

This chapter considers the challenges that higher education faces in taking up this expanded obligation. I discuss two main assertions that seem particularly important for future progress. The first is that real understanding of students' progression in education will remain fragmented until we can bring together, within a common framework, theories of learning, development, and instruction. Understanding how people learn, how the intellect changes

NEW DIRECTIONS FOR TEACHING AND LEARNING, no. 109, Spring 2007   © Wiley Periodicals, Inc.
Published online in Wiley InterScience (www.interscience.wiley.com) • DOI: 10.1002/tl.262

over time, and how to effectively design and implement a course or curriculum is not the same as knowing how knowledge in each of these areas can work together.

The second assertion concerns how we put new knowledge about student learning and development to work. Unless we can envision more effective change processes for faculty and administrators—that is, support their own learning and development—the best prediction we can make about students becoming cognitively mature and secure in their identities and relationships is that they will have to continue working it out largely on their own. In a sense, the shape and pace of their development is dependent on the shape and pace of our development.

Both assertions deserve careful elaboration, which I approach based on two perspectives. First, as an educational psychologist, I have spent many years attempting to put teachers, or prospective teachers, in touch with research on learning in ways that are meaningful and potentially useful. This movement of ideas from research frameworks to practice environments is never easy, and there is much we still need to learn. Second, and even more pertinent to this discussion, is my role and work during the past ten years as director of a university teaching center. One of our longest-running projects during those years has been a collaborative effort with Marcia Baxter Magolda to integrate student development concepts into our thinking about undergraduate education at Virginia Tech (Wildman, 2004). One outcome of this broader project is the two-year integrated curriculum discussed in Chapter Five in this volume by Barbara Bekken and Joan Marie, in which the concept of self-authorship plays a central role. What is not fully explained in the description is an entire subplot, which essentially is about how they managed to pull off the work they have accomplished given the considerable odds against success. A good deal of that story relates to the need for a better understanding of how learning and developmental concepts come together in new instructional models and how people can learn to implement these new practices.

There is some good news about my two assertions and also some cautionary elements to consider. The good news is that much work has already been done to explain the connections between research on adult intellectual development and instructional practices that support such development. The persistent and enlightening work of Baxter Magolda (1992, 1999b) and others in carrying forward and expanding Robert Kegan's notion (1994) of self-authoring, and in particular the articulation of concrete principles of instructional engagement using the Learning Partnerships Model (LPM; Baxter Magolda and King, 2004), truly does provide the elements of a road map for educational change. Furthermore, some preliminary tests of this new road map are producing promising results for students (see Chapters Five and Six, this volume).

Nevertheless, the cautions we need to keep in mind are perhaps as important for future progress as is the available good news. First, the inevitable progress we will see in better coordinating research related to development, learning, and instruction is going to produce additional complexity for practitioners. In higher education, we are accustomed to working with basic and predictable goal structures related to student outcomes, usually expressed in terms of knowledge and skill acquisition. The transmission or dissemination models typically used to convey knowledge allow faculty members to enact a relatively safe technical practice, drawing as necessary from research and theory (behavioral and cognitive) showing how knowledge and skill development best proceeds. The addition of student development goals to the mix creates levels of uncertainty and instability that essentially require a reframing of what it means to engage in professional instructional practice. Faculty members will now be thrust into a reflective mode that is inventive in nature, decidedly nontechnical, and ultimately disruptive to the bureaucratic systems that were designed to nurture the standard technical practice. Educators who decide to take student intellectual development seriously, even with the guidance of good advice such as provided with Baxter Magolda's learning partnerships framework, will be thrust into the dual mode of adjusting their own teaching behavior while seriously negotiating institutional requirements that were likely not put in place with the idea of students taking charge of their own education. These complicating conditions may explain why successful implementations to date are so often pilot projects or initiatives located in contexts such as graduate schools, honors programs, especially cohesive academic departments, or other special contexts that tend not to threaten the mainline instructional delivery machinery in our institutions.

When we speak of taking the intellectual growth of students seriously, I believe we are talking about mainstream education, and not simply demonstration projects that live on borrowed time, uncertain resources, and the extraordinary efforts of a few pioneers. To accomplish this broader impact, we will need to reframe what we mean by learning and instruction, find ways to learn and live with increasingly nontechnical instructional practices, and remove institutional barriers. The importance of a new storyline—a new script for negotiating learning in schools—cannot be overemphasized. Interventions that run counter to cultural expectations tend to be short-lived because the energy required to overcome settled practice is so significant and relentless. The bottom line, suggested in the title of this chapter, is that self-authorship will require serious professional and institutional accommodations.

Linking Development, Learning, and Instruction

The patterns of intellectual development that occur during the college years have been well documented (see, for example, Belenky, Blythe, Goldberger, and Tarule, 1986; Baxter Magolda, 1992; King and Kitchener, 1994; Perry, 1968), yet these descriptive accounts are only potentially useful for education. We may be troubled by evidence that first-year college students see knowledge as mostly fixed truths created by others, but the findings themselves only dimly illuminate a process for stimulating further growth toward higher-level functioning such as self-authorship. Indeed, these descriptive accounts may simply verify what we have long taken for granted: that intellectual growth, like student motivation, for example, is yet another complicating but largely uncontrollable factor in the education process. What is needed is a more coherent storyline showing the interconnections among learning, development, and instruction.

Several obstacles need to be addressed in developing this fuller story. One difficulty is that the significant research contributions in each of these areas (learning and student development) have developed in parallel rather than as a holistic and coordinated project. Second, the literatures in these areas are reaching different audiences. Indeed, our institutions are organized around professionally distinct groups (for example, academic and student affairs) who frame their worlds separately and have professionalized their roles based on their own special knowledge bases. This professional distinctiveness is enhanced and reinforced through campus structures and national associations that play to these separate identities. Is this a problem? A recent study, *Learning Reconsidered: A Campus-Wide Focus on the Student Experience,* undertaken by the National Association of Student Personnel Administrators and the American College Personnel Association (2004), would seem to suggest that it is. This entire monograph is devoted to the claim that all of higher education needs to rethink the traditional dichotomies that divide responsibility for student learning across various institutional precincts.

To digress slightly here, during the period in which I was preparing for writing this chapter, I was also engaged in teaching a graduate course I developed some years ago dealing with research on human cognition and relationships with instructional practice. The course reading material typically includes dozens of articles and chapters chosen to bring students into contact with the most influential researchers and writers, ranging from the onset of the cognitive movement in the late 1950s to the present time. When I encountered *Learning Reconsidered* and began thinking about its purpose, I was eager to see how the mainstream research on cognition and situated cognition may have been reflected in the reference list of this interesting work. What I tentatively guessed was quickly confirmed: there were no sources in common. The reverse is true as well: very little, if any, of the mainstream learning research my students were reading referenced the developmental literature of primary interest in the student affairs domain. If I wanted my students to see this research, I would need to look outside the typical sources that address learning theory, which I did for a portion of the course. The task we then faced was how to place the relevant concepts from these different literatures on the same page, so we could fashion a coherent view of learning and learners. This is not a simple process, even with time and resources to devote to the task.

A different issue arises even if our divergent professional groups were inclined to be on the same page. This is the matter of how we convey knowledge to busy practitioners. When the findings from research in the domains of learning, development, and instruction are distilled and compiled for practitioners, what we typically find is a rather daunting array of abstract propositions that are difficult to understand as a coherent story and rarely point to a coherent plan for action.

Two such compilations of findings from research on learning during the past fifteen years exemplify efforts to inform schooling practice. In 1993 the Presidential Task Force on Psychology in Education of the American Psychological Association summarized twelve learning principles in *Learner-Centered Psychological Principles: Guidelines for School Redesign and Reform*. In 1998 the American Association for Higher Education, the American College Personnel Association, and the National Association of Student Personnel Administrators produced their own report, *Powerful Partnerships: A Shared Responsibility for Learning*, which presented ten learning principles for consideration. It is quite common for practitioners to acquire information about learning from relatively brief listings of the important points or themes. The orientation in these presentations generally reflects a cognitive bent; we are reminded that learners actively construct meaning, that existing knowledge is crucial to future learning, that there are individual variations and motivations that influence learning potential, and that learning is contextual and often social in nature. Given that we have been working on this research for a good fifty years, there are quite a lot of details to share beyond these major themes.

Notably, in each of the summaries mentioned, only a nod is given to learning as a developmental process. Expressed in the form of a single principle in each list, development essentially becomes one more thing to consider alongside multiple other dimensions of learning. Educators who may be interested in finding out how learning relates to development are essentially left to figure the story out on their own. Indeed, given the fragmentary nature of most such presentations, designed to give busy professionals a peek at important research findings, the successful reader will likely be the one who comes already equipped with a well-developed schema for this research, ready to engage in top-down processing. The individual who is less conceptually prepared will experience greater difficulty making sense of the whole.

A more extensive and widely cited resource on learning research comes from the National Research Council's 1999 study, *How People Learn: Brain, Mind, Experience, and School*. This more extensive discussion of learning research includes a chapter on intellectual development in early childhood and makes the case that learning and development should be viewed as integrated, not parallel, interests. The authors clearly show that intellectual development is critical to understanding how children make sense of and interact with their environments, and in particular they show how changes in conceptual growth occur. The case is also made that children comprehend very early how their own minds work and how to control their own learning activities through metacognitive strategies. Research is also cited, as a caution to teachers, that early on, some children may adopt a view of their own intelligence as fixed, in contrast to others who believe intelligence is malleable and can be increased. The critical point about these beliefs is that even at an early age, children react more or less productively to potential learning situations based on assumptions they make about their own intelligence. Specifically, what is at stake is whether children come to see their educational experiences from a learning perspective or a performance (compliance) perspective.

However, in the manner of textbook treatments of complex topics, subsequent chapters in *How People Learn* move on to other topics, and the importance of developmental trajectories is not worked all the way through. Specifically, this compilation of learning research does not report on intellectual development during the early adult years. So, again, despite the tremendous value and popularity of this particular resource, there is much left for practitioners to work out for themselves with respect to intellectual growth.

Self-Authorship and Learning

The general idea now emerging is that theories of learning and intellectual development (self-authorship) should do more than coexist in parallel frameworks; rather, they should bootstrap each other in the service of schooling practices that view student development and learning as part of the same overall growth trajectory. In this section, I briefly point to some of the common ground that should allow such a view.

Readers should keep in mind that what we know about learning has been a moving target and continues to change and evolve. Since the 1950s, we have seen at least three major theory shifts that propose dramatically different conceptions of learning, ranging from behavior analysis, to information processing, to cultural participation. Each of these frameworks for explaining learning suggests its own particular conception of the learner, and over time we simply come to see learners in quite different roles.

Behaviorally, learners are subject to conditioning through the systematic reinforcement of particular behaviors in particular contexts. Complex behaviors can thus be acquired using applied behavior management techniques, and real competence in valued activities can result. Critics argue, perhaps unfairly, that conditioning puts the learner in a strictly passive role, but that is an argument for another time. With the beginning of the cognitive revolution, learning, which could be broadly defined in terms of the construction of meaning (see Bruner, 1990), was increasingly seen as something the learner does rather than something that happens to the learner. In essence, learning itself became an acquired commodity the learner could own, could become good at, and could develop an identity around. Learning could be incidental or purposeful, private or social, and could best be seen as a constructive or developing process.

Within the cognitive framework, knowledge development plays a central role and is seen as complex and evolving into specialized memory architectures. Common architectural forms include scripts, schemas, and conceptual networks. The basic idea is that humans naturally create representations of experience that capture not so much the details but the essential meanings they will need to negotiate further experience. For example, visits to the doctor, the dentist, the pastor, the teacher, the sporting event, the wedding, the graduation ceremony, and thousands of other culturally important events are coded in terms of the regularities of these events that give them meaning, and these coded scripts allow future visits to proceed with predictability and comfort. Stories too are remembered not verbatim, but in terms of story schemas that allow us to easily traffic across stories, remember them, and even make them up when needed.

Part of the mystery of learning is the question of how we move from relatively naive, shallow, or incorrect representations to scripts and schemas that are more complex and suitable for the world yet to be discovered. It turns out this is very much the developmental mystery faced along the route to self-authorship. How do we create the conditions that cause students to change their minds—to give up an early set of epistemic beliefs in favor of more advanced beliefs about the nature of knowledge? If these questions about learning and development were of a totally different order, then we might expect the mechanisms supporting change to differ as well. Yet the change mechanism we talk about with our learning hat on is virtually identical to the change processes we look to when wearing our developmental hat. The basic sense of it emanates from the Piagetian notion of conceptual conflict or disequilibrium. The basic idea is that humans tend to modify their beliefs or conceptual structures when these beliefs are no longer compatible with new evidence. This fundamentally basic idea has been elaborated by Dole and Sinatra (1998) from a cognitive psychology perspective and by Bendixen and Rule (2004) from the perspective of personal epistemology.

Continuing the story just briefly, knowledge, in whatever state of construction, leads to other desired outcomes, such as perception, comprehension, further knowledge development, problem solving, and continuing development of one's identity as a learner and participant in cultural endeavors. All of these cognitive activities are more or less under the control of the learner, and when there is conscious awareness of how the process is going and deliberate application of strategies to correct difficulties, we say the learner is behaving metacognitively. The learner behaving metacognitively understands there is something to know about knowing and using knowledge. This realization and skill tends to separate people in terms of school success, but fortunately it is a commodity that can be shaped and cultured in learners.

We have also recently come to realize that learning can be thought of in ways that do not presuppose knowledge to be the privileged commodity. Learning outside of schools, within the cultural activities of daily life, is thought to focus more on the particular roles that people acquire, and the identities they develop, as practitioners (see, for example, Lave and Wenger, 1991, and Wenger, 1998). Master practitioners will certainly be seen as knowledgeable, but knowledgeable in the sense of their total adaptation to a domain of practice. Within everyday cultural practices, there is no assumption that explicit verbal knowledge is necessary for application to future contexts. Rather, it is knowledge in practices situated within a lived-in world that is of most value. Such knowledge is communicated narratively and tends to be codified not in the kinds of propositions that appear in texts, but in the stories that are common within families, work groups, or professional communities. One of the interesting features of Baxter Magolda's longitudinal study, as well as some of the other special pilot projects she and others speak of, is the prevalence of stories. These more complex settings for learning apparently involve a more complete adaptation to challenges and situations that can best be conveyed narratively. In contrast to the more computationally oriented cognitive models, stories are not simply confined to addressing knowledge and skill; they also include intentions, feelings, commitments, strategies for resolving dilemmas, and the like. In his provocative book *Acts of Meaning,* Jerome Bruner (1990) reminds us that learning is about the construction of meaning, and despite what he refers to as cognitive psychology's preoccupation with individual computation of information, we should never assume that learners can be separated from their cultural world and realize their full powers. His meaning is clear in the statement that "a failure to equip minds with the skills for understanding and feeling and acting in the cultural world is not simply scoring a pedagogical zero, it risks creating alienation, defiance, and practical incompetence" (p. 43).

Judging Learning Theory by the Company It Keeps

In spite of the fact that researchers have been so industrious for so long in the learning arena, they have left a large gap between the questions of how knowledge and skill develop and how human beings themselves develop as intelligent participants in world. If the research programs oriented to how we build knowledge and performance capacity in people are deemed incapable of answering questions about how we influence personal epistemologies and identities as knowers, is that the fault of the knowledge base itself or the way in which we have typically interpreted and applied knowledge about learning? Why is it that we seem enriched with such elegant descriptions of how development occurs but stuck in such a complete mystery about what to do about it?

I propose that we are better equipped than we may think, based on developments in learning research, to design environments that simultaneously address developmental needs along with the more traditional learning needs that are typically of concern in academic courses and curricula. Part of the justification for this assertion is that typical schooling scripts actually draw on and use only a fraction of what we know about human learning. In the process of thinking about learning within such a constrained frame, we have imposed quite severe penalties on imagining what is possible.

Recitation and teaching by telling is confirmed by research to be the dominant script for instructional practice in American schools. This has been the case for nearly a hundred years. While we may use other terms, such as *lecture* or *direct instruction*, the processes involved in recitation are familiar to every citizen. This script for teaching and learning holds the teacher responsible for knowledge delivered, tasks undertaken, questions posed, and assessments of progress in learning.

Within this narrow yet dominant conception of instructional practice, learning research has proven to be useful, but only a fraction of the available horsepower is actually needed. Thus, if the dominant market for learning research is the schooling enterprise, and the dominant schemes for schooling privilege a particular use for learning research (support of the recitation script), then we may easily overlook other applications, such as support of concepts like self-authorship, which are not typically articulated as the chief aims of schools. In a sense, we have engaged in a type of self-handicapping in which our expectations for learning research have been seriously diminished.

Moving from Knowing That to Learning How

Knowing how to conceptualize learning, development, and instruction as a single unit of analysis is a good beginning. The more daunting challenge is to learn how to implement models of instruction that are consistent with the major premises underlying self-authorship. How are these new goals to be implemented? What is the process for encouraging and supporting instructional faculty to learn and implement teaching practices that represent significant departures from the status quo?

During the past decade or so, we have seen dozens of major studies indicating the increasing gap between what we know about student learning and development and the dominant instructional and curricular practices that characterize existing school cultures. The problem seems to be that as our knowledge of learning and development changes, classroom practices are generally stuck in the same gear—based in the same script that has dominated education across generations. Studies that have looked historically at teaching practices point to continuing reliance on a few commonplace instructional activities, guided by mostly commonsense notions about student development and learning. As Derek Bok points out in his recent book, *Our Underachieving Colleges* (2006), there continues to be an overwhelmingly conservative bias in instruction methodology, with upward of 70 to 80 percent of faculty members continuing to rely on the lecture or some close variation as the mainstay of their teaching. These numbers are consistent with a survey conducted at my own institution during a study in which we were attempting to forecast classroom designs for the future.

Faculty learning and adaptation is a major consideration as we consider potential mainstream adoption of instructional approaches that do not follow the usual schooling script, such as would be the case with the learning partnerships model. As Baxter Magolda (1999b) has herself described, the model presents a daunting challenge even for professors who have conceptually assimilated the right moves that need to be taken. Barbara Bekken and Joan Marie report similar challenges in Chapter Five in this volume, even with the support of a university teaching center, their own small faculty learning community, and continuing direct advice from Baxter Magolda. In their struggles to implement a four-semester integrated curriculum. they identified their own need for the evolutionary bridge that Kegan (1994) describes as necessary to connect students to new ways of thinking. Whether the metaphor is bridge building or border crossing (Baxter Magolda, 1999b), the essential theme is the same: the adaptation to new teaching methodologies is complex and must be thought of as a learning problem in its own right—one that is conceptually similar to the developmental changes and interventions we are proposing for students. Before we discuss interventions, however, it will be useful to briefly consider how these deeply rooted understandings of instructional practice were formed in the first place.

If we return for a moment to the conditions that gave rise to the familiar patterns of teaching and learning, which many now recognize must change, we should understand that these patterns were born out of direct experience. We acquire our initial sense of schooling practices as we would learn the regularities of any other cultural activity, such as visiting a restaurant, going to a doctor, taking a trip, or negotiating a romance. As each experience unfolds, we abstract from it the main defining features and store these features as a representation of the experience. The importance of all such scripts or schemes is that they give structure and meaning to our lives; these structures allow us to carry out our affairs with predictability and reasonable degrees of comfort. In the case of schooling, even the youngest of participants quickly develop for themselves an in-the-head account of how school goes. These accounts are continually updated and refined with ongoing experience, and importantly, they are shared with others as narratives of the practice of schooling. It is important to note that there is no direct telling in this; the learning is experiential, and it is powerful.

This adaptation to schools is also more complex than simply knowing what schools are about and how to negotiate the tasks presented in classrooms. As Carl Bereiter (1990) points out, schools are richly contextual and involve extensive adaptations on the part of children. Hence, there are additional components to students' overall adaptation to school that may involve affect, identity or persona, problem adjustment strategies, and codes of conduct. Bereiter is thus suggesting that children undergo an early and massive adaptation in which schoolwork is seen as a job to be undertaken—a type of social practice in its own right. Given that the entire structure of schools is designed to support and reinforce this adaptation, it is unlikely that participants would develop scripts at odds with the norm.

As we examine the workings of schools, it becomes clear that they constitute one of the most culturally powerful and pervasive experiences that virtually all citizens share. Within this universally shared activity, a shared narrative develops that conveys the core meanings of school experience and contains all of the cognitive and emotional entailments that are needed to create lasting impressions and commitments.

The role and purposes of teaching in schools are clearly a central part of the cultural image of schools. Experiences with teaching will vary, of course, but the central tendency in Western society is to organize schools where "human beings deliberately teach each other in settings outside the ones in which the knowledge being taught will be used" (Bruner, 1996, p. 20). The universal methodology for this is telling, questioning, and testing (Finkel, 1999; Tharp and Gallimore, 1988), where "individual and presumably omniscient teachers explicitly tell presumably unknowing students something they presumably know nothing about" (Bruner, 1996, p. 20). Following repeated exposure to salient examples of this culturally sanctioned practice, a deeply embedded image of teaching is created that no amount of telling will dislodge.

By the time college students enter their respective institutions, they will have completed more than a decade-long apprenticeship in the art and practice of school going. During this time they will have completed more than twenty thousand academic tasks and will have amassed significant experience in academic skills such as note taking, chapter outlining, test taking, strategic reading for tests, paper writing, and performance of laboratory exercises. Mastering these skills is an important part of the total adaptation to school, although they may be largely irrelevant to performance in the relevant domains referenced by the academic tasks. Even worse, what is gotten across through these instructional tasks and arrangements for learning may have little to do with the movement toward self-authorship.

Instructional faculty in colleges and universities are themselves subject to these dominant cultural images of teaching and learning. They have experienced the same apprenticeships in schools, and, largely self-taught in the practice of teaching, they have had no reason or way to acquire alternative scripts. Moreover, their script-governed activities are seldom subject to disruption, given the bureaucratic supports available and the fact that students are working from the same script, and perhaps even demanding it.

Border Crossing for Faculty

What we are now asked to imagine is a change process for faculty that will counteract what is a deeply embedded cultural image of teaching, schools, and student engagement. The purpose of the preceding paragraphs was to provide some background on the nature of the complete adaptation that has taken place, so we can make realistic assessments of how to proceed to implement a new model. Clearly, the learning partnerships model poses quite different assumptions about knowledge development than would be characteristic of a schoolwork script, and the accompanying instructional principles suggest entirely new relationships with students, basically extending to them a full partnership role in knowledge construction. The question then is how to proceed.

The difficulty with script change (read also as conceptual change) is that direct instruction—telling—will not work. The scripts that govern teaching and learning in most college classrooms were acquired through experience, not telling, and hence change strategies will need to include direct experience. Several ingredients seem necessary. First, the complexity of constructivist-type instruction, which is posed as a basic requirement of the learning partnerships model, cannot be easily mastered alone. Assistance will be required as newcomers to the methodology attempt to frame and implement entirely new interactions with students. It is simply not possible to imagine such change based on verbal instruction alone. Second, the assistance provided will need to occur within authentic activity structures. This essentially means dedicating real classrooms as laboratories for faculty learning. Third, within this environment, the apprenticeship relationship should take on a pattern that is decidedly developmental in nature. This means that not only is technical assistance provided, such as modeling a certain type of classroom discourse process, but the goal is also to guide the apprentice to reinvent conceptions of learning and teaching through assistive dialogue. The aim of such assistance is to move the apprentice toward increasingly self-guided performance, which over time may become completely internalized and automatic.

We do not normally think in these terms with respect to faculty development. A more typical approach is to employ for faculty a close approximation of the models they typically use for student learning. That is, we organize workshops designed to convey information verbally that may be used for instructional improvement. We are enticed into this by the dominant script for teaching and encouraged by the fact that verbal propositions in their stripped-down versions are simple and easy to package and deliver.

The analysis and suggestions offered here are certainly not of my own invention. Some readers may have recognized the distinctly Vygotskian concept of assisted performance in this discussion. In this case, I am drawing from the work of Tharp and Gallimore (1988), expressed in their influential book *Rousing Minds to Life: Teaching, Learning, and Schooling in Social Context*. Their originating concern in producing the book is that schools actually do very little teaching—that the ubiquitous recitation script is designed primarily to train students how to deliver factual answers to satisfy relatively low-level questions flowing from the school's curriculum objectives. Within this framework, students would rarely be provided assistance in developing elaborated ideas requiring reformulation of existing concepts.

Tharp and Gallimore essentially propose a reframing of teaching and schooling based on Vygotsky's transformative ideas (1978) about the relationships between learning and development (see also Moll, 1990). Vygotsky's signature concepts were to recognize children as active agents in the educational process and, more important, demonstrate that instruction must be arranged so that learning processes effectively lead development. Specifically, he proposed that a fundamental step in the educational process is to recognize that zone of proximal development, where a child might perform at an incrementally higher level given proper assistance. The process would involve the child's being offered a difficult goal, then attaining that goal with adult assistance, and then achieving independence from the adult through the guidance of self-talk and self-mentoring. Over time, the process repeats, with the child engaging in a process of internalizing the social process to achieve a new level of consciousness.

This process of assisted performance is equally adaptable for support of adult performance and development and would involve the same series of stages. The initial step is to have the novice engage the desired teaching practice in a supportive environment (activity setting), where more capable peers or mentors can provide the assistance needed to negotiate the task at hand. In this context of assisted activity, the novice may be asked to perform routines or activities beyond his or her current repertoires and perhaps discrepant from existing beliefs. Over time, the assistance provided by others is replaced by self-guidance and inner speech.

The activity setting may involve planning, classroom instructing, working with individual students, assessing performance, or any other activity that is an authentic part of the overall instructional context. During the period of high mentor regulation, the novice will be an authentic coparticipant but may not fully understand the way that goals are being formed, transactions with students are being negotiated, and flow of activity is being managed. Through discussion and dialogue, the novice gradually comes to acquire some concept of the activity, and gradually a degree of intersubjectivity with the mentor will emerge. As this happens, the mentor or peer is able to use his or her significant arsenal of supportive strategies (such as modeling, cognitive framing, questioning, feedback, and contingency managing) to move the novice to the point where other-assistance can be withdrawn and self-assistance can take over (see Tharp and Gallimore, 1988, for a more complete discussion).

Following these two stages of direct assistance, resulting in increased self-regulation, the performance will become internalized through ongoing practice and application. As with any other complex skill, there is the possibility of performance regression—perhaps with changes in context—and the mechanisms of earlier stages may need to be reinstated.

Clearly the image of development as a simple unfolding process is a less than satisfactory metaphor. For adults who teach, the stakes for getting it right are high. The proposal offered here is to deliberately employ for professional practice the same processes for rousing minds to life that are used with children and young adults. If there is any chance of overcoming the inertia of existing instructional models, we will need an explicit curriculum, based on sound theory about learning and development.

Taking Intellectual Development Seriously

Sometimes the truth can slip out quite innocently. During an extended discussion of issues related to the university's core curriculum and its contribution to student learning outcomes, a respected senior professor remarked on how fortunate it is that we matriculate students at age eighteen and graduate them at age twenty-two or twenty-three. Stated more as a tension reliever at the end of a long day, this observation may contain more truth, or perhaps hopeful anticipation, than we care to admit. In the absence of a rich concept of intellectual growth, is it possible that we simply assume that development takes care of itself as a by-product of maturation (that is, getting older)? Or might we assume that development does require special assistance of the type provided primarily by student affairs programs, leaving the academic sector free to focus on the acquisition of increasingly complex general and disciplinary and professional knowledge bases?

In either case—assuming that development happens automatically as a by-product of increasing age or that someone else is responsible for nudging it forward—the question of intentionality is raised. The key question is suggested in the chapter title: Are we really serious about student intellectual development? As we consider the specific concerns and assertions outlined here, it may be useful to hold in mind some of the indicators that something is being taken seriously in higher education.

Certainly one indicator that a process or outcome is valued is that we see tangible signs of commitments to that process or outcome. Such commitments are expressed in institutional goals, included in strategic plans, and visible in the ways in which we think and talk about these outcomes on our campuses. Resources are generally committed to processes and outcomes we take seriously; they tend not to be allocated for outcomes we take for granted, even if those expected outcomes are deemed highly desirable.

We tend to have benchmarks in mind for outcomes we take seriously. In institutions that focus heavily on research, close attention is always paid to grant dollars, research expenditures, and publications. Metrics are in place to assess performance in such areas. We tend to know with some precision the square footage of office space needed, the number of classroom seats required, the bandwidth required for technology applications, and the timeliness with which departmental bills are paid. On the business side of our work, tangible reinforcement is provided when performance meets or exceeds expectations. Things that we take seriously get noticed. Institutionally we know how to take seriously a very large range of processes and outcomes. Think about fundraising, for example. Institutions that take fundraising seriously tend to follow their graduates and potential patrons over a lifetime. Performance is measured not simply by what we do today but what we can put in place for the future.

Finally, those things we really take seriously generally show up as indicators for career advancement. For faculty members, the promotion and tenure process is a prime place to look. Here we do not simply take it for granted that one will publish, present, bring in funds, and teach a certain load; we measure it directly, and there is usually continuing speculation about how much is necessary for success. In essence, we know how to take things seriously in higher education. Thus, it is a fair expectation that real commitments to the intellectual life of our students will be a visible part of the institutional landscape.

References

American Association for Higher Education, American College Personnel Association, and National Association of Student Personnel Administrators. *Powerful Partnerships: A Shared Responsibility for Learning.* Washington, D.C.: American Association for Higher Education, American College Personnel Association, and National Association of Student Personnel Administrators, 1998.

Baxter Magolda, M. B. *Knowing and Reasoning in College.* San Francisco: Jossey-Bass, 1992.

Baxter Magolda, M. B. *Creating Contexts for Learning and Self-Authorship.* Nashville, Tenn.: Vanderbilt University Press, 1999a.

Baxter Magolda, M. B. "Learning-Centered Practice Is Harder Than It Looks." *About Campus,* 1999b, 4(4), 2–4.

Baxter Magolda, M. B. "Self-Authorship as the Common Goal of 21st Century Education." In M. B. Baxter Magolda and P. M. King (eds.), *Learning Partnerships: Theory and Models of Practice to Educate for Self-Authorship.* Sterling, Va.: Stylus, 2004.

Baxter Magolda, M. B., and King, P. M. (eds.). *Learning Partnerships: Theory and Models of Practice to Educate for Self-Authorship.* Sterling, Va.: Stylus, 2004.

Belenky, M., Blythe, C., Goldberger, N., and Tarule, J. *Women's Ways of Knowing: The Development of Self, Voice, and Mind.* New York: Basic Books, 1986.

Bendixen, L. D., and Rule, D. C. "An Integrative Approach to Personal Epistemology: A Guiding Model." *Educational Psychologist,* 2004, 39(1), 69–80.

Bereiter, C. "Aspects of an Educational Learning Theory." *Review of Educational Research,* 1990, 60(4), 603–624.

Bok, D. *Our Underachieving Colleges: A Candid Look at How Much Students Learn and Why They Should Be Learning More.* Princeton, N.J.: Princeton University Press, 2006.

Bruner, J. S. *Toward a Theory of Instruction.* New York: Norton, 1966.

Bruner, J. S. *Acts of Meaning.* Cambridge, Mass.: Harvard University Press, 1990.

Bruner, J. *The Culture of Education.* Cambridge, Mass.: Harvard University Press, 1996.

Dole, J. A., and Sinatra, G. M. "Reconceptualizing Change in the Cognitive Construction of Knowledge." *Educational Psychologist,* 1998, 33(2/3), 109–128.

Finkel, D. L. *Teaching with Your Mouth Shut.* Portsmouth, N.H.: Boynton/Cook, 1999.

Kegan, R. *In over Our Heads: The Mental Demands of Modern Life.* Cambridge, Mass.: Harvard University Press, 1994.

King, P. M., and Kitchener, K. S. *Developing Reflective Judgment: Understanding and Promoting Intellectual Growth and Critical Thinking in Adolescents and Adults.* San Francisco: Jossey-Bass, 1994.

Lave, J., and Wenger, E. *Situated Learning: Legitimate Peripheral Participation.* Cambridge: Cambridge University Press, 1991.

Moll, L. C. (ed.). *Vygotsky and Education.* Cambridge: Cambridge University Press, 1990.

National Association of Student Personnel Administrators, American College Personnel Association. *Learning Reconsidered: A Campus-Wide Focus on the Student Experience.* Washington, D.C.: National Association of Student Personnel Administrators, American College Personnel Association, Jan. 2004.

National Research Council. *How People Learn: Brain, Mind, Experience, and School.* Washington, D.C.: National Academy Press, 1999.

Perry, W. P. *Forms of Intellectual and Ethical Development in the College Years: A Scheme.* Austin, Tex.: Holt, 1968.

Presidential Task Force on Psychology in Education, American Psychological Association. *Learner-Centered Psychological Principles: Guidelines for School Redesign and Reform.* Washington, D.C.: American Psychological Association, 1993.

Tharp, R. G., and Gallimore, R. *Rousing Minds to Life.* Cambridge: Cambridge University Press, 1988.

Vygotsky, L. S. *Mind in Society: The Development of Higher Psychological Processes.* Cambridge, Mass.: Harvard University Press, 1978.

Wenger, E. *Communities of Practice: Learning, Meaning, and Identity.* Cambridge: Cambridge University Press, 1998.

Wiggins, G. P. *Assessing Student Performance.* San Francisco: Jossey-Bass, 1994.

Wildman, T. M. "The Learning Partnerships Model: Framing Faculty and Institutional Development." In M. B. Baxter Magolda and P. M. King (eds.), *Learning Partnerships: Theory and Models of Practice to Educate for Self-Authorship.* Sterling, Va.: Stylus, 2004.

TERRY M. WILDMAN is assistant provost for faculty development and assessment, and also serves as director of the Center for Excellence in Undergraduate Teaching at Virginia Polytechnic Institute and State University in Blacksburg, Virginia.

3

Institutional and programmatic effectiveness in promoting self-authorship requires an understanding of how to assess self-authorship.

Assessing Self-Authorship

Jane Elizabeth Pizzolato

Beginning with Perry's description of patterns (1968) in college students' intellectual development, scholarship on the epistemological development—students' beliefs about and processes for knowledge construction—of college students has focused on clarifying how epistemological development unfolds (Baxter Magolda, 1992; Belenky, Clinchy, Goldberger, and Tarule, 1986; King and Kitchener, 1994) and what facilitates development and demographic differences in development (Baxter Magolda, 1992, 2001; Belenky, Clinchy, Goldberger, and Tarule, 1986; Bing and Reid, 1996; Pizzolato, 2003).

The most recent addition to the literature on epistemological development was Baxter Magolda's introduction (2001) of empirical evidence for self-authorship, a way of knowing originally described by Kegan (1994). From interview data collected as part of her longitudinal study of ways of knowing, Baxter Magolda (2001) found a significant shift in epistemological orientation as her participants moved into postcollegiate roles and contexts. Until this point, her participants had learned to seek and follow formulas and even recognize that knowledge was contextually bound—that is, what counted as right or wrong or good or bad depended in large part on the context. In romantic relationships, on the job, and in graduate school, her participants encountered expectations that they make decisions and act in ways that required an integration of personal values and goals with formal logic and the goals, values, and beliefs espoused by others, disciplines, and institutions. In response to the mismatch between their actual ways of knowing and those required of them, students sought to clarify their own goals, values, and

NEW DIRECTIONS FOR TEACHING AND LEARNING, no. 109, Spring 2007 © Wiley Periodicals, Inc.
Published online in Wiley InterScience (www.interscience.wiley.com) • DOI: 10.1002/tl.263

beliefs and then enact them in ways that balanced them with their cognitive understanding of logic and the role of context in knowledge construction.

Baxter Magolda (2001) termed the process of questioning, clarifying, and finally enacting their goals, beliefs, and values the process of self-authorship. As a three-phase journey, students moved from questioning (the crossroads), to clarifying (becoming the author of their own lives), to acting in ways that integrated the intrapersonal and cognitive in interpersonal arenas (internal foundations). Although the first two phases imply significant movement toward self-authorship, it is in the third phase, internal foundations, that students are truly coming to know from a self-authored perspective. Self-authorship can thus be defined as an orientation to knowledge construction and evaluation based on balancing an understanding of the contextual nature of knowledge with intrapersonally grounded goals, beliefs, and values.

Promoting Self-Authorship: The Learning Partnerships Model

From her examination of how her participants developed self-authorship, Baxter Magolda (2001) claimed self-authorship could be facilitated in college students through implementation of her Learning Partnerships Model (LPM). The LPM is grounded in three principles: validate learners as knowers, situate learning in learners' experiences, and define learning as mutually constructing meaning. In practice, these principles mean that instructors and student affairs professionals should present a variety of perspectives for understanding and interpreting situations, problems, and texts and then support students' use of varied perspectives to develop and defend their own understandings. By pushing students to develop their own beliefs, teachers and student affairs professionals can help students see that they are capable of making sense of complexity: their experience, and the self more generally, is important to knowledge construction, and knowledge is socially constructed.

Practices designed to promote self-authorship are one important part of the process of enhancing college students' epistemological development. However, if institutions or programs wish to assess their effectiveness in promoting self-authorship, it seems important that appropriate assessment tools be developed for this purpose. Currently there are no measures of self-authorship development separate from interviews used in research studies on self-authorship development (Baxter Magolda, 1992, 2001; Creamer and Laughlin, 2005; Lahey and others, 1988). Consequently, existing program design and evaluation work related to self-authorship development has relied on use of one of three options in assessing movement toward self-authorship, and student change in a learning partnership environment: (1) use of existing measures to approximate cognitive change (Hornak and Ortiz, 2004), (2) use of a survey or scoring measures designed to examine student outcomes in the context under scrutiny (Haynes, 2004; Piper and Buckley, 2004), or (3) reliance on semistructured interviews and reading student narratives, such as journal entries or reflection papers, with a small sample of participants (Egart and Healy, 2004; Yonkers-Talz, 2004). Although these methods have provided rich descriptions of practices designed to support movement toward self-authorship and students' experiences in them, it is hard to determine if progress toward self-authorship has been made and what type of progress it is—in large part because the existing measures were not designed to assess self-authorship and the literature on self-authorship has focused more on describing development than deconstructing the orientation into measurable chunks. Developing a short, quantitative measure of self-authorship would allow assessment of student development and consequently could be used in program evaluation. Furthermore, such a measure could be used to look at correlative change on other skills or attitudes such as self-regulation or intercultural competence. The remainder of this chapter describes one measure of self-authorship, reviews its development, and outlines possible practical uses.

The Self-Authorship Survey

The Self-Authorship Survey (SAS) is half of a two-part measure of self-authorship. The other half is a questionnaire, The Experience Survey (ES), which will be discussed in the following sections. The SAS is a twenty-four-item Likert-type instrument comprising four subscales: Capacity for Autonomous Action, Problem Solving Orientation (PSO), Perceptions of Volitional Competence, and Self-Regulation in Challenging Situations (SRC). Together these subscales provide an estimate of students' developing self-authoring abilities. Looking more closely at what self-authorship is fosters discussion of how the subscales work individually and collectively to measure self-authorship.

According to Baxter Magolda (2001) and Kegan (1994), self-authorship comprises three dimensions: cognitive, intrapersonal, and interpersonal. The cognitive dimension accounts for how students know—that is, students' beliefs about the nature of knowledge (Does knowledge change over time, or is it fixed? Are there universal truths? Or is knowledge more contextual and culturally bound?) and their role in knowledge construction (Is knowledge received from authorities? Or is knowledge socially constructed? Are knowledge construction processes formulas or heuristics?). The cognitive dimension is the most often-studied dimension of epistemological development in the college student literature, and so measurement of this dimension is not unique. Perry (1968), Belenky, Clinchy, Goldberger, and Tarule (1986), and Baxter Magolda (2001) all focused their investigations around interview questions that sought to understand how students conceptualized and engaged in knowledge construction (the cognitive dimension) within educational contexts.

Although the cognitive dimension is certainly important to understanding epistemological development, studies of self-authorship suggest it typically develops and is displayed in out-of-class experiences (Baxter Magolda, 2001; Pizzolato, 2003, 2005a). In Baxter Magolda's participants (2001), for example, self-authorship development often arose from a need to define oneself separate from expectations held by parents or significant others, or in relation to expectations at work that had real consequences for participants and others important to them. Questions of "Who am I?" "What do I value?" and "Why?" all became increasingly important to these participants, and as they sought to define themselves and then align their reasoning and action with these internal definitions, they moved toward self-authorship. These questions "Who am I?" and "What do I value?" are at the crux of the intrapersonal dimension of self-authorship—the dimension that recognizes the influence of identity on epistemology.

The final dimension is the interpersonal dimension. In this dimension, self-authored students have moved from relying on others for self-definition, direction, and beliefs to developing healthy relationships where they can learn from others without being unduly influenced by them. Others can be consulted in ways that honor external perspectives and opinions while also recognizing the potential in their own ideas, opinions, and abilities.

Defining self-authorship as multidimensional and specifying the dimensions is helpful in understanding how self-authorship and assessment of it connect to existing constructs and measurement tools. The cognitive dimension could be measured using existing measures of intellectual development. The intrapersonal dimension could be measured using identity measures, and autonomy instruments could measure the interpersonal dimension. The trouble with such a measurement practice or even with compiling items from existing scales is that this method likely will not capture the essence of self-authorship. Because self-authorship integrates the three dimensions in reasoning and acting, measuring the dimensions separately seems inappropriate, whether using separate existing measures or developing items for each dimension's scale. Furthermore, such assessment practices can speak only to shades of presence or absence of self-authorship along any of the dimensions. To be a truly helpful tool, an instrument should assess the degree of development in a way that informs practice. Said otherwise, if an instrument measures subsets of skills underlying a particular developmental construct, then assessment should speak to movement toward the goal outcome in a way that identifies which skills need improvement. Consequently, the SAS was developed by deconstructing the dimensions into skill sets (problem-solving skills, relationships with authorities, volitional competence, autonomy) by drawing on theoretical analysis and conversations with scholars and then factor-analyzing the items. The resulting four factors were named for the unifying skill they tapped: Capacity for Autonomous Action (six items), Problem Solving Orientation (eight items), Perceptions of Volitional Competence (six items), and Self-Regulation in Challenging Situations (four items). The

SAS and its subscales have been shown to have strong internal consistency and test-retest reliability. Table 3.1 describes each subscale, provides sample items, and gives reliability information (see Pizzolato, 2005b, for information on the scale's development).

Using the Scale

Using a five-point Likert-type scale for each item, students (N = 991) completing the SAS were instructed to think carefully about each statement and mark the degree to which they agreed or disagreed with the statement based on the way they usually thought and acted. The scale provides two scores: subscale scores and a total self-authorship score obtained by averaging the subscale scores. The higher the score is, the greater is the likelihood that the student can reason and act in self-authored ways.

Table 3.1. Test-Retest Reliability and Internal Consistency for SAS Subscales

Scale or Subscale	Sample Items	Test-Retest Reliability	Alpha
Capacity for Autonomous Action	I tend to make decisions based on what people I admire think is best, even if it isn't always what I think is best. (r)	.91**	.81
	If my friends are doing something I don't want to do, I often do my own thing without them.		
Problem-Solving Orientation	Some people, especially authority figures—teachers, adults, coaches—often have better opinions and ideas than I do. (r)	.82**	.80
	When I'm making decisions I spend time thinking about how my decision fits with my goals and principles.		
Perceptions of Volitional Competence	When I set a goal for myself, I come up with a specific plan of how I'm going to achieve it.	.92**	.81
	When I set a goal for myself, I'm pretty sure I'm going to be able to achieve it.		
Self-Regulation in Challenging Situations	When things start getting hard, I often have trouble sticking with my plans. (r)	.84**	.73
	I often have trouble breaking real life problems down into smaller parts. (r)		
SAS scale		.87**	.88

Note: **p < .01

Students also completed the Experience Survey, which asked them to write narratives about an important decision they had made. A series of prompts helped students construct complete narratives—for example, "Why did you have to make this decision?" "What were your options?" "What did you decide to do?" "What did your decision-making process look like?" and "Would you make the same decision today?" These prompts were based on those used in interviews to help participants illustrate how they constructed knowledge and made decisions. Because self-authorship involves (1) the ability to reason in ways that foster engaging in multiple perspectives in a way that simultaneously honors one's own internally defined goals, beliefs, and values, and (2) action congruent with such reasoning, decision making seemed an appropriate arena in which to assess self-authorship because it also involves reasoning (considering options) and action (making a decision).

Student responses to the survey were scored on a scale of one to four on three domains (decision making, problem solving, and autonomy) used to assess self-authorship in interview methods. Increases in scores on each domain represented qualitatively different skill sets that showed closer approximation to those expected to be displayed in self-authoring students. Consequently a positive relation between students' scores on the ES and the SAS should suggest the SAS may be able to measure self-authorship in college students. Two coders participated in coding 25 percent of the responses to establish inter-rater reliability (decision making: $\kappa = .76$, problem solving: $\kappa = .84$; autonomy: $\kappa = .92$; see Pizzolato, 2005b, 2006, for further discussion of the ES).

Examination of the relation between student scores on the SAS and the ES, however, added another wrinkle to understanding self-authorship assessment: the correlations between SAS scores and codes from the ES were only modest ($\rho = .51$, $p < .01$). The correlation was significant, which implies that the SAS may be able to accurately measure self-authorship in college students, but since the correlation was only at .51, there is an underlying implication that the two measures are not as related as initially hypothesized. Investigation into why the correlation was not as high as expected led to three important findings and two assessment implications.

In open-ended questioning formats like the ES, students were able to choose to discuss an experience that was highly important to them but in which they were not an actor. Instead they were affected by actions of others. In other words, students were able to discuss important experiences where they were not in control of enough pieces of the situation to be required to use highly complex epistemological orientations. For example, one student talked about stopping riding. This decision came not through any decision to stop on her part but rather because her father sold her horse. Certainly this was a memorable experience, and possibly an important one, but it was not one that required complex processing on her part. Her cognitive processing in this case was limited to processing the reality that her father sold her horse and so she could not ride it anymore. There was no evidence that her processing involved reflection or action related to her goals or beliefs. Consequently, the student's reasoning and action were not found to be representative of self-authorship. Although it is certainly possible that the student had not yet developed self-authoring abilities, it is also possible that the measure did not effectively tap whether and the degree to which she was moving toward self-authorship. Because she was not asked to discuss how she behaves typically, she may have chosen to discuss a moment of great importance to her but not one that is representative of her typical ways of being and knowing. The difference in what students had the opportunity to consider on the SAS and the ES varied, and consequently students who chose to write about important experiences where they were not actually making decisions tended to display significantly fewer signs of self-authorship when assessed using the ES as compared to the SAS.

Similarly, the ES asked students to describe an important decision they had made. In response, some students said they had never made an important decision or any decision at all. These responses did not allow coding for self-authorship other than to say that there was no evidence of self-authorship. Such a score flew in the face of the students' scores on the SAS. On that measure, students were not asked to consider a specific moment but rather their general or typical ways of knowing and being. The SAS provided them with options of not being in control of making decisions; reliance on others was assessed through items such as, "I often can't do things if people I admire think I shouldn't" and "Some people, especially authority figures—teachers, adults, and coaches—often have better opinions and ideas than I do." Furthermore, because of the way the SAS was constructed—to assess skills underlying each dimension necessary for self-authored reasoning and action—it allowed item analysis to understand possible reasons that students who said they had not made any important decisions had not regardless of whether the obstacles were related to cognitive development (Problem Solving Orientation) or underdeveloped levels of autonomy, volitional competence, or self-regulation.

A third important finding was the discrepancy between student scores on the SAS and the ES based on student word choice. This was particularly an issue with students who wrote about faith-based decisions such as accepting Christ or being born again. Consistent use of language like "surrendering" or "turning things over to the Lord" suggests dependence on faith in a way that more closely resembles formula following rather than a healthy relationship where they understand the role of free will in even strict fundamentalist beliefs. On the SAS, students were asked to specify the degree to which their beliefs were internally defined (for example, "When I think about my principles and morals, I know I've spent a lot of time figuring out why I believe these things"). And this issue of figuring out why they believe what they do was separated from figuring out what they believed, a process represented by different items. The SAS thus allowed examination of the degree of reflectiveness brought to faith and its enactment in a way that remained obscured behind word choice in the narratives.

Although these examples seem to support the SAS as a more accurate or utilitarian tool for measuring self-authorship than a method that focuses on rich description of a single or few situations, there were certainly instances where students' responses to the ES demonstrated signs of self-authorship not apparent or not as strong in their responses to the SAS. I attribute this reality to a possibility hypothesized in the construction of the ES. Because it measures self-authorship in a moment of significance to the student, it may be more likely to call on the student's most complex epistemological skills—skills that the student may not typically use (as is measured on the SAS).

An additional benefit to using the ES with the SAS was that the survey was able to richly highlight the reasoning-action split in self-authorship. For example, Bree's decision to return to her predominantly white institution after being accepted as a transfer student to a historically black college (HBC) demonstrates the split between reasoning and action. Her processing of the situation showed signs of self-authored reasoning. She considered her options, and the benefits and consequences of each, and assessed the implications of these options based on her own goals for herself and what she thought would ultimately be best for her in the situation: "I could come back and be a mentor [resident assistant] or go to an HBC in the South where I eventually want to live and become part of the majority again." Despite her ability to reason in ways suggestive of self-authorship, Bree did not transfer to the HBC because her parents decided she was going to stay where she was. This example implies that whether students can act in self-authored ways may depend in part on whether the situation they find themselves in is supportive of self-authorship. Bree could reason in self-authored ways, but her decision, coupled with her statement that "my parents made the decision," does not seem self-authored. The inconsistency between her reasoning and action may be due to her perception that her situation did not permit self-authorship or that the cost of self-authorship would be too great. If her parents decided she was staying, it is certainly possible that if she chose to exert her self-authoring abilities, she could have faced serious repercussions from her parents.

On the surface, this does not appear to be a display of self-authorship, but if self-authored reasoning is separated from self-authored action, it has more potential to be viewed as self-authoring for two reasons. First, there is evidence that Bree processed her decision-making situation in ways suggestive of self-authored reasoning. Second, in his fifth order of consciousness, self-authorship, Kegan (1994) emphasizes that self-authorship does not mean such knowers always get what they want but privileges the embracing of complexity of situations and identities.

Furthermore, because decisions are made within the context of relationships, with the limitation of time, and in the context of both immediate and long-term goals, it seems appropriate to hypothesize that students who show signs of self-authored reasoning but choose to act in ways seemingly inconsistent with their reasoning may in fact be making a decision that shows signs of self-authorship in an arena larger than the immediate decision. This seems particularly possible in traditional college students who live on campus. Such students are in the midst of relational transition with their families and are encountering new peers as they enter and move through college. Thus, while some of the mismatches in reasoning and action may be due to an absence or still emerging self-authorship ability, others may be a function of the developmental context. Students are shifting roles in stable contexts (as in the family) and shifting between contexts (from home to school, for example), and so they are likely privy to an array of perspectives on any situation or topic. Purely based on probability, students may sometimes stumble onto an idea they agree with, and so in their compliance it may look as if they have followed a directive from another.

Finally, given the importance of and power differential inherent in parent-child relationships even when the children are college students, it seems possible that adolescents and college students may sometimes find self-authored action too risky to enact, especially if they are living in their parents' house or are financially dependent on their parents. In an attempt to balance their own development and goal achievement with the maintenance of healthy relationships with their parents, college students may make choices that appear to negate their reasoning skills. Therefore, they may make choices that appear not to be self-authored if the assessment context is limited to the decision itself. If the context is broadened to include the many roles, contexts, and decisions any college student is balancing at once, it seems plausible that what appears not to be self-authored in the immediate context is actually quite self-authored on another level. Following a thorough assessment of options and implications, coupled with reflection on internally defined beliefs, goals, and values, students may make decisions that change in apparent degree of self-authorship depending on the scope of the context in which it is considered:

- Implication 1. Given the potential importance of options assessment, self-authorship may be best considered situational. Whether students act on self-authored reasoning may be related to the degree to which they perceive the situation to be supportive of self-authorship. Here, *supportive* means that self-authored action will not have a negative impact on students' ability to maintain or reach other personal, professional, or relational goals in excessive amounts. The importance of options assessment in self-authored action suggests that while self-authorship development may be linear, once a self-authored orientation has been developed, actual public expression of this orientation may be situational.
- Implication 2. The idea of situational self-authorship, coupled with the function of context framing in self-authorship assessment, leads to four potential expressions related to self-authorship. These expressions of self-authorship are outlined in Table 3.2.

Table 3.2. Self-Authorship Expression Matrix

	Self-Authored Action	*Non-Self-Authored Action*
Self-Authored Reasoning	*Expression 1:* Action consistent with reasoning; both action and reasoning evidencing self-authorship	*Expression 2:* Action inconsistent with reasoning; action appears non-self-authored, but reasoning shows signs of self-authorship
Non-Self-Authored Reasoning	*Expression 3:* Action inconsistent with reasoning; action suggestive of self-authorship, but underlying reasoning ability not present	*Expression 4:* Action consistent with reasoning; neither action nor reasoning indicative of self-authorship

Expression 4 is clearly not self-authored on any level, but the other three expressions have the potential to be identified as self-authoring. Whether self-authorship is assessed by behavior or reasoning skills, students falling into expression 1 will be identified as self-authoring, because both their reasoning and actions are consistent with the self-authored orientation. Students falling into expression categories 2 and 3, however, may be misidentified depending on the form of assessment used. Students grouped in expression 2 may make decisions that seem inconsistent with their reasoning because options assessment leads them to choose options other than their initially preferred option.

With expression 3, if self-authorship is assessed by behaviors, some students may be classed as self-authoring, when in fact they cannot reason in self-authored ways. Without the underlying ability to cognitively synthesize intrapersonal goals, sense of self, and epistemic assumptions, action cannot be self-authored, because it is not being guided by internal foundations but rather by gut instinct, rebellious desires, or a desire for satisfaction or amusement. For example, a student who makes a decision to reject her parents' desire for her to be a math major and instead pursue a journalism major may or may not be self-authoring in this decision. If the student makes this decision because she truly wants to be a journalist, has thought out the implications of this decision, and, following some reflection on the implications of this decision, has gone through the process of switching majors, she may be self-authoring. If, however, the student makes this decision purely to be rebellious, then it is not a self-authored decision. Without knowledge about the motivation behind the decision, actions may be labeled self-authoring when they are not. In understanding motivation, then, it is important to clarify what students mean when they use words or phrases like "want" or "best for me," because they can signify independent knowing or self-authored knowing. If a student wants to do something because it feels right, it is independent knowing. If a student wants to do something because it is most consistent with internally defined goals, it is more likely to be self-authoring.

In addition to misidentifying students based on reasoning-action incongruence, it also seems important to emphasize the importance of assessing self-authorship by both reasoning and action so that students who self-author through actions consistent with others' expectations are not misidentified. Although self-authorship typically may emerge or be displayed through actions that separate students from the majority, important others, or community principles, this may not always be the case. Although it is likely less frequent, students may act in self-authored ways while still acting in ways consistent with community standards and expectations of authority figures.

Together the SAS and the ES seem to meet these needs. The SAS provides a reasonable and statistically sound measure of self-authorship in a way that can be used as both a summative and formative evaluation, because it provides both a measure of self-authorship and an identification of strengths and weaknesses relative to skills underlying self-authorship. The ES builds on the SAS by providing insight into how the reasoning-action split may play out in individual students. Thus, until an even stronger measure of self-authorship is developed, using the two in conjunction seems best able to serve the diverse needs (such as program evaluation, student outcome assessment, or diagnostic testing) of postsecondary institutions and programs attempting to facilitate self-authorship development in students.

References

Baxter Magolda, M. B. *Knowing and Reasoning in College: Gender Related Patterns in Students' Intellectual Development.* San Francisco: Jossey-Bass, 1992.

Baxter Magolda, M. B. *Making Their Own Way: Narratives for Transforming Higher Education to Promote Self-Authorship.* Sterling, Va.: Stylus, 2001.

Belenky, M. F., Clinchy, B. M., Goldberger, N. R., and Tarule, J. M. *Women's Ways of Knowing: The Development of Self, Voice, and Mind.* New York: Basic Books, 1986.

Bing, V. M., and Reid, P. T. "Unknown Women and Unknowing Research: Consequences of Color and Class in Feminist Psychology." In N. Goldberger, J. Tarule, B. Clinchy, and M. Belenky (eds.), *Knowledge, Difference, and Power: Essays Inspired by Women's Ways of Knowing.* New York: Basic Books, 1996.

Creamer, E., and Laughlin, A. "Self-Authorship and Women's Career Decision-Making." *Journal of College Student Development,* 2005, *46*(1), 13–27.

Egart, K., and Healy, M. P. "An Urban Leadership Internship Program." In M. Baxter Magolda and P. King (eds.), *Learning Partnerships: Theory and Models of Practice to Educate for Self-Authorship.* Sterling, Va.: Stylus, 2004.

Haynes, C. "Promoting Self-Authorship Through an Interdisciplinary Writing Curriculum." In M. Baxter Magolda and P. King (eds.), *Learning Partnerships: Theory and Models of Practice to Educate for Self-Authorship.* Sterling, Va.: Stylus, 2004.

Hornak, A. M., and Ortiz, A. M. "Creating a Context to Promote Diversity Education and Self-Authorship Among Community College Students." In M. Baxter Magolda and P. King (eds.), *Learning Partnerships: Theory and Models of Practice to Educate for Self-Authorship.* Sterling, Va.: Stylus, 2004.

Kegan, R. *In over Our Heads: The Mental Demands of Modern Life.* Cambridge, Mass.: Harvard University Press, 1994.

King, P. M., and Kitchener, K. S. *Developing Reflective Judgment.* San Francisco: Jossey-Bass, 1994.

Lahey, L., and others. *A Guide to the Subject-Object Interview: Its Administration and Interpretation.* Cambridge, Mass.: Harvard University School of Education, Subject-Object Research Group, 1988.

Perry, W. P. *Forms of Intellectual and Ethical Development in the College Years: A Scheme.* Austin, Tex.: Holt, 1968.

Piper, T. D., and Buckley, J. A. "Community Standards Model: Developing Learning Partnerships in Campus Housing." In M. Baxter Magolda and P. King (eds.), *Learning Partnerships: Theory and Models of Practice to Educate for Self-Authorship.* Sterling, Va.: Stylus, 2004.

Pizzolato, J. E. "Developing Self-Authorship: Exploring the Experiences of High-Risk College Students." *Journal of College Student Development,* 2003, *44*(6), 797–812.

Pizzolato, J. E. "Creating Crossroads for Self-Authorship: Investigating the Provocative Moment." *Journal of College Student Development,* 2005a, *46*(6), 624–641.

Pizzolato, J. E. "Assessing Self-Authorship." Paper presented at the American Educational Research Association, Montreal, Quebec, Canada, 2005b.

Pizzolato, J. E. "Complex Partnerships: Self-Authorship and Provocative Academic Advising Practices." *NACADA Journal,* 2006, *26*(1), 32–46.

Yonkers-Talz, K. "A Learning Partnership: U. S. College Students and the Poor in El Salvador." In M. Baxter Magolda and P. King (eds.), *Learning Partnerships: Theory and Models of Practice to Educate for Self-Authorship.* Sterling, Va.: Stylus, 2004.

JANE ELIZABETH PIZZOLATO is an assistant professor of applied developmental psychology at the University of Pittsburgh.

NEW DIRECTIONS FOR TEACHING AND LEARNING • DOI: 10.1002/tl

4

Decisions that involve consideration of inconsistent or contradictory information provide a context for understanding and supporting intellectual development.

Engaging Differences: Self-Authorship and the Decision-Making Process

Anne Laughlin, Elizabeth G. Creamer

Our conceptualization of the relationship between decision making and self-authorship evolved over the course of a five-year project exploring the process that young women use to make career-related decisions (Creamer, Burger, and Meszaros, 2004; Creamer and Laughlin, 2005; Meszaros, Creamer, Burger, and Matheson, 2005). Self-authorship offers a theoretical lens to understand the meaning-making processes that individuals use to make a wide range of decisions (Baxter Magolda, 2004). It is linked to decision making because it influences how individuals make meaning of the advice they receive from others and the extent to which the reasoning they employ reflects an internally grounded sense of self (Baxter Magolda, 1998, 1999, 2001).

Over five years, our interdisciplinary research team collected several waves of qualitative and quantitative data related to self-authorship and the career decision-making process. By the time we approached the end of the project, we had interviewed more than a hundred high school and college women, along with sixty of their parents, and analyzed data from over thirteen hundred responses to three iterations of our questionnaire. Not surprisingly, given the quantity and variety of our data, numerous discrepancies emerged during data analysis between quantitative and qualitative responses supplied by the same participant, and also within interviews as

This project received support from the National Science Foundation (grant 0120458).

participants responded to questions about self-authorship that on the surface seemed quite similar. Although our initial inclination was to dismiss these data as unreliable, further discussion over the course of eighteen months proved valuable in developing new ways of thinking about self-authorship. As we grappled with contradictions that emerged during data analysis, implications for participants' intellectual development and our own approach to inquiry became apparent.

In this chapter, we draw from the self-reported experiences of our participants and a reflexive account of our own inquiry to examine insights that may emerge from efforts to make meaning of discrepant information and advice. We use the lens of self-authorship to interpret findings from our study of the career decision-making process in a group of college women and weave this together with a reflexive account of our own decision-making process as researchers.

Our consideration of decision making breaks the process into three phases that individuals move through in an iterative process: (1) gathering information from various sources, including self and others; (2) considering how to manage information to reach a decision; and (3) reflecting on the outcome of the decision and changing or reaffirming future decision-making processes through learning or development. The first two phases are reflected in Baxter Magolda's definition of self-authorship as "the ability to collect, interpret, and analyze information and reflect on one's own beliefs in order to form judgments" (1998, p. 143). The third phase reflects an implicit assumption of constructive developmental theories, like self-authorship, that "people actively construct or make meaning of their experiences—they interpret what happens to them, evaluate it using their current perspective, and draw conclusions about what experiences mean to them" (Baxter Magolda, 2004, p. 31). According to this view, developmental transformation requires self-reflection and results from the interaction of internal thoughts or assumptions and external experiences (Baxter Magolda, 2004).

Engaging Difference in Personal Decision Making

Studies by multiple theorists over a period of more than thirty years have shown a similar pattern of development characterized by the shift from near total reliance on authority figures as the source of knowledge to a place where individuals can consider multiple views to make their own decisions about knowledge claims (Baxter Magolda, 1992; Belenky, Clinchy, Goldberger, and Tarule, 1986; Kegan, 1994; King and Kitchener, 1994; Perry, 1968). This research indicates that individuals at different points in the developmental continuum handle each phase of the decision-making process outlined above in recognizably different ways. Individuals early in the developmental journey, who make meaning based on external formulas, would be expected to seek answers from authority and to uncritically follow the advice of others perceived to know the right course of action. Those who are at the midpoint of the journey are likely to have recognized the importance of making decisions that are not heavily influenced by authorities but have yet to actualize their mental framework. Those much further along on the developmental journey would be characterized by the capacity to consider information and advice from diverse sources and integrate them with internally defined values and beliefs before ultimately making their own decision. A key feature of self-authored decisions is the willingness to engage diverse viewpoints without losing perspective of one's own values and beliefs.

Engaging Difference in Research

In educational research, the most common approach to mixed methods is to use quantitative and qualitative data in a complementary fashion to answer different questions (Patton, 2002). The drawback of this approach is that it allows researchers to avoid confronting inconsistencies in their data while ignoring the point that differences are to be expected. Patton (2002) has noted that "researchers using different methods to investigate the same phenomenon should not expect the findings generated by these different methods to automatically come together to produce some nicely integrated whole" (p. 557). In team-driven research, debates over divergent findings from the analysis of quantitative and qualitative data can be reduced to paradigmatic squabbles, disciplinary differences, or dichotomous judgments about which source of data to give most credence. Another way of looking at mixed methods is to consider each inquiry tradition as revealing some different aspect of empirical reality. This approach is not simply a quest for convergence or agreement among different sources of data, but for the credibility that arises from grappling with different interpretations or hypotheses. Patton observes, "Areas of divergence open windows to better understanding of the multifaceted, complex nature of phenomenon" (p. 559).

Within qualitative research traditions, there are a number of conventional ways to include the exploration of differences in analysis, including through triangulation, negative case analysis, sampling to achieve maximum variation, and the consideration of alternative hypotheses. These methods do not simply add credibility to the study but also have the potential to strengthen and deepen theoretical insight.

The Women in Information Technology Project

The findings presented here are based on a subset of data from the initial stages of a five-year study that used questionnaire and interview data to explore the relationship between self-authorship and women's career decision making. This project, funded by the National Science Foundation, focused on women's decisions related to careers in information technology, a field in which women are traditionally underrepresented. The initial questionnaire was completed by 117 women (almost half self-identified as a racial or ethnic minority) who were enrolled in one of four universities in Virginia. It gathered information about the participants' career-related decisions, including sources of career-related information and advice. We later completed telephone interviews with forty of these women using a semistructured interview protocol designed to elicit information about the process that they went through to decide on an academic major or career. The interviews were transcribed verbatim and used to expand and deepen our understanding of the factors that influenced the student's decision-making process. Our interest was neither the actual career choice nor the behavior of seeking input but the meaning-making processes that occurred as individuals considered, disregarded, or simply chose not to engage different points of view while making a significant personal decision with long-term consequences.

We approached the analysis of our quantitative and qualitative data concurrently, so that each of us was informed by the other. Before coding each transcript, we sought a context for interpreting the interview by reviewing the participant's replies to key questions on the questionnaire. This strategy alerted us to a fairly consistent pattern of discrepancies. Although we did not anticipate the striking differences we encountered among our interview and questionnaire data, we believe that our pursuit of them has led to some important insights about the links between our participants' intellectual development and their decision-making process, as well as about conducting research using the theoretical framework of self-authorship.

Students: Inconsistencies and the Journey Toward Self-Authored Decisions. We used both the questionnaire and the interview to ask participants about the role others had played in their career decision-making process. These questions elicited information about the degree to which participants relied on external authority versus an internally developed sense of self, as well as the extent to which they considered multiple perspectives before making important decisions, both indicators of self-authorship. In the questionnaire, we asked participants to rate how often they spoke to different groups of people about careers; we also asked if friends and parents had significantly influenced their decisions. In the interviews, we asked if there were people who had significantly influenced our participants' career decisions and how those people had been influential.

As we examined the qualitative and quantitative data, we detected inconsistencies in participants' responses about who they turned to for career-related advice. Most participants indicated on the questionnaire that they discussed careers at least a few times with a wide range of people, including friends, parents, family members, advisors, and teachers. In contrast were the qualitative responses in which participants rarely identified advisors, teachers, or professional role models as being influential as they made their decisions. Of the college women responding to our questionnaire, 86 percent indicated that they had discussed career plans with a counselor or advisor, yet only 7 percent of the women interviewed said that a counselor or advisor had significantly influenced their career interests.

The first finding to result from our analysis is that when students speak with others about important decisions such as career choice, there appears to be a significant distinction between whom they talk with and whose advice they seriously consider (Creamer and Laughlin, 2005). Although questionnaire responses indicated that participants had consulted a variety of people, the questionnaire failed to distinguish between the act of hearing advice and the act of seriously considering that advice, a distinction noted by a number of our participants during interviews. Conversely, the interview responses helped us to understand whose advice was most influential, but it failed to show the full variety of people who were consulted. An example of this distinction is a participant who indicated on the questionnaire that she discussed her career plans with a variety of people, including her advisor, friends, and siblings. In the interview, she refers only to the influence of conversations with her parents and boyfriend: "My parents' opinions are important simply because I know they would only give me advice on the basis of love, and my boyfriend's opinion holds a little bit of power simply because I see a future with him, but ultimately the most important would probably be my parents and myself."

After asking participants about whose advice was important to them, we asked why they considered opinions from these people important. The most common reply had to do with the participant's sense that the people giving advice (in most cases, parents) cared for her and would know what was best for her. For example one woman stated, "Just because I trust them [parents and sister], I know that they are looking out for my best interests, they're not going to tell me something that is going to hurt me." Another participant explained, "Because they're my parents and I think they know what's best for me sometimes." Rarely did participants go beyond an explanation based on personal regard or say anything that would imply that they were making judgments about the credibility of the information or the experience of the person giving advice. For a large majority of participants, we interpreted the criteria they used for considering someone's advice to be the nature of the personal relationship they had with that person rather than any judgment about the person's knowledge or expertise.

Another contradiction occurred between the responses referring to parents in the quantitative and qualitative data. Only 15 percent of the college women responding to the questionnaire agreed that their decisions were strongly influenced by their parents; however, 98 percent of the women interviewed listed parents among those whose opinions were important to consider when making significant decisions. A typical example was one of our participants who strongly disagreed on the questionnaire that her parents influence her decisions; however, when asked in the interview (without any reference being made to the questionnaire) if anyone's opinions were important to her when making a big decision, she said, "My mother, because she's always supported me in everything, and if she doesn't like something, then I'm kind of iffy; I've got to be iffy about it."

A conclusion that came from our exploration of this kind of contradiction is that students in the early phases of self-authorship may be extremely sensitive to societal expectations that they make their own decisions even while they still rely heavily on the advice of trusted others. Baxter Magolda (2004) has similarly described the experience of some of her longitudinal participants who recognized that they had to make decisions for themselves yet continued to rely on external formulas. A statement from one of our college women provides an example of this kind of newly realized independence coupled with acknowledgment of the effort required to act in new ways:

> My sisters and I, they go to different schools, and so that whole thing of separation from them was a huge thing for me, coming to college here and learning to be on my own as an individual person, and just overcoming that bond I had with them because we're not together anymore. . . . Being independent is a big thing nowadays, . . . learning to stand your ground, and be on your own and do things on your own for yourself, without having to rely on other people to tell you an answer, or tell you when you have to do this and that.

Several participants indicated in both the questionnaire and the interview that they believed their choices were independent, while also pointing in the interview to the importance of personal relationships in shaping their decisions.

Another difference related to students' confidence in their decision-making ability. Among our participants, 63 percent agreed, or strongly agreed, that they were sure about their ability to make a career decision. Contrasting with this relatively high level of confidence were the responses to a question in our interview protocol asking the participant how she would respond if someone suggested a career option that was different from what she had already considered. Responses seemed to reflect conviction about the importance of deciding for themselves, although their full statements often implied that they had foreclosed on their choice and would not consider advice that contradicted what they had already decided. For example, one woman stated: "I would listen to whatever the person had to say, but if I'm pretty much stuck on what I want to do, then it doesn't really matter what they have to say, I mean I'll take it into consideration and what they have to say might be valid, but I already have my mind made up."

Reluctance, if not inability, to genuinely consider input from diverse others emerged as a key theme across interviews. We noted that participants' confidence in their own ability to make independent choices did not necessarily reflect the capacity to decide on their own after genuinely considering multiple perspectives, a hallmark of self-authored decisions. High levels of decision-making self-confidence may be the result of simply committing to a choice, whether that decision involved first considering multiple options or not. Accordingly, it is not a contradiction for an individual to have a high level of self-confidence about her emerging independence while simultaneously lacking the capacity to consider advice involving a variety of views. Indeed, one possibility is that the presence of self-confidence in decision making may facilitate progression away from reliance on external authority.

Researchers: Engaging Differences in Data Analysis. Consideration of apparent differences between questionnaire data and interview data produced some important conclusions. First, participants made a distinction between whom they consulted about career options and who actually was influential to them. Second, the reason most often cited for listening to advice related not to the expertise or credibility of the person offering the advice but to the nature of the relationship. Finally, students may express confidence in their ability to make independent decisions while maintaining a heavy reliance on the advice of close others. Using the lens of self-authorship, we interpret each of these findings as characteristics of students' operating from the early phases of the journey toward self-authorship.

The use of mixed methods proved valuable in our research, not just to confirm findings through the convergence of data but also for the insights that resulted from our efforts to reconcile different types of data. With self-authorship as our theoretical lens, we began to see similarities between the decision-making process of our participants and that of our research team. The participants made meaning of different information and advice related to career decisions, while we made meaning of different, and sometimes seemingly conflicting, information from research data. Most participants chose to believe some advice (for example, that provided by close others) while disregarding other advice. By contrast, as researchers, we chose not to dismiss one type of data as more credible than another. We considered several possibilities: that differences might be due to subtle differences in wording, that some or all of our data could be invalid, and that each method has particular kinds of bias. While acknowledging these possibilities, we had no evident reason to believe that any of them provided the best explanation for our results; therefore, we looked for a way to make sense of the data as a whole. We view this kind of integration as a form of self-authored analysis because it involves seriously considering multiple perspectives and possibilities before ultimately deciding what to believe based on the evidence in context.

Conclusion

In our study, the deliberate attempt to integrate quantitative and qualitative data created the opportunity for more nuanced thinking about self-authorship and self-authored decision making. The theory of self-authorship provided a useful framework for understanding the processes that our participants used to make major decisions, including the way they made meaning of information and advice. Our findings indicate that simply exposing students to divergent views and sources of knowledge, without supporting true engagement with those views, may not be the most effective way to foster development because students may not be open to considering perspectives that differ from their own. Complex thinking requires recognition of one's own personal role in meaning making, a step that is preceded by recognition that knowledge is socially constructed (Baxter Magolda, 1999). This transition is aided by discussions about the limits of knowledge and authority. However, classroom observation indicates that communication about the uncertainty of knowledge is infrequent in the language teachers use in the classroom (Chandler, Hallett, and Sokol, 2002). To promote more complex thinking, particularly about career options, educators may need to reconsider the language and value assigned to certainty and decisiveness. Communicating that there are multiple possible answers for ill-structured problems, highlighting areas where knowledge is uncertain, and suggesting that uncertainty and skepticism are qualities that often characterize advanced thinkers are ways that educators can set the stage for the development of complex decision-making skills.

A major step in students' developmental journey is learning how to determine and use appropriate criteria to judge the quality of information and advice. Our findings indicate that students who lack this ability may use the nature of their personal relationships with others as a criterion for judgments, thereby reinforcing their dependence on external authority. Educators in general, and student affairs personnel in particular, may need to rethink the way they work with students' parents and close others. If college students are continuing to rely heavily on their parents for advice about academic and career decisions, it may be appropriate to focus significant efforts on educating parents about the importance of their role in supporting their student's move toward more self-authored decision making.

Our work indicates that for academic and career advisors, focusing attention on the process students use to make important personal decisions is an effective way to open communication about developmental growth. The topic is also manageable within the context of an individual advising session or class. Educators working with students who express confidence in their academic and career decisions may find, on probing, that the decision-making process students are using does not include serious consideration of a wide variety of alternatives. Questions about the process, rather than the outcome, of decision making are more likely to reveal students' advising needs from a developmental perspective. In addition, we found that our participants were considerably more articulate and comfortable when recalling their thoughts related to a real-life decision that was personally meaningful to them than when answering a more abstract question about how they approached decision making in general. By working with students to reflect on their own decision-making process and also about what a self-authored decision might look like, educators may promote the development of self-authorship in other areas of life as well.

References

Baxter Magolda, M. B. *Knowing and Reasoning in College: Gender-Related Patterns in Students' Intellectual Development*. San Francisco: Jossey-Bass, 1992.

Baxter Magolda, M. B. "Developing Self-Authorship in Young Adult Life." *Journal of College Student Development*, 1998, *39*(2), 143–156.

Baxter Magolda, M. B. *Creating Contexts for Learning and Self-Authorship*. Nashville, Tenn.: Vanderbilt University Press, 1999.

Baxter Magolda, M. B. *Making Their Own Way: Narratives for Transforming Higher Education to Promote Self-Development*. Sterling, Va.: Stylus, 2001.

Baxter Magolda, M. B. "Evolution of a Constructivist Conceptualization of Epistemological Reflection." *Educational Psychologist*, 2004, *39*(1), 31–42.

Belenky, M., Clinchy, B., Goldberger, N., and Tarule, J. *Women's Ways of Knowing: The Development of Self, Voice, and Mind*. New York: Basic Books, 1986.

Chandler, M. J., Hallett, D., and Sokol, B. W. "Competing Knowledge Claims About Competing Knowledge Claims." In B. K. Hofer and P. R. Pintrich (eds.), *Personal Epistemology: The Psychology of Beliefs About Knowledge and Knowing*. Mahwah, N.J.: Erlbaum, 2002.

Creamer, E. G., Burger, C. J., and Meszaros, P. S. "Characteristics of High School and College Women Interested in Technology." *Journal of Women and Minorities in Science and Engineering*, 2004, *10*(1), 67–78.

Creamer, E. G., and Laughlin, A. "Self-Authorship and Women's Career Decision-Making." *Journal of College Student Development*, 2005, *46*(1), 13–27.

Kegan, R. *In over Our Heads: The Mental Demands of Modern Life*. Cambridge, Mass.: Harvard University Press, 1994.

King, P. M., and Kitchener, K. S. *Developing Reflective Judgment: Understanding and Promoting Intellectual Growth and Critical Thinking in Adolescents and Adults*. San Francisco: Jossey-Bass, 1994.

Meszaros, P. S., Creamer, E. G., Burger, C. J., and Matheson, J. "Mothers and Millennials: Career Talking Across the Generations." *Kappa Omicron Nu FORUM*, 2005, *16*(1). Retrieved Dec. 1, 2006, from http://www.kon.org/archives/forum/16-1/meszaros.html.

Patton, M. Q. *Qualitative Research and Evaluation Methods*. (3rd ed.) Thousand Oaks, Calif.: Sage, 2002.

Perry, W. P. *Forms of Intellectual and Ethical Development in the College Years: A Scheme*. Austin, Tex.: Holt, 1968.

ANNE LAUGHLIN *is a doctoral candidate in educational leadership and policy studies at Virginia Polytechnic Institute and State University in Blacksburg, Virginia.*

ELIZABETH G. CREAMER *is a professor in educational research and evaluation at Virginia Polytechnic Institute and State University in Blacksburg, Virginia.*

5

Making self-authorship a goal of an interdisciplinary multisemester general education program shows great promise for meeting desired undergraduate learning outcomes for citizen-learners.

Making Self-Authorship a Goal of Core Curricula: The Earth Sustainability Pilot Project

Barbara Bekken, Joan Marie

Survival in the 21st century requires flexibility, adaptability, the capacity to negotiate between one's own and others' needs, and the ability to cope with rapid change, ambiguity, diversity, and complexity.

—M. B. Baxter Magolda (2001, p. xxi)

As earth and environmental science educators, we have spent the past two decades addressing resource-related issues: from the burning of fossil fuels, to concerns over clean water, to potential disruptions in the climate-regulating flow of the ocean's currents, to the deleterious effects of a rapid increase in atmospheric carbon dioxide levels. Over the years, we have become concerned as literally hundreds of students have dismissed appeals to commit to greater responsibility in creating a more sustainable future as they focused instead on their goal of checking off yet another distribution requirement. How could they not care deeply about these issues? What could we do to engage students so that they would become effective citizens able to cope with the complexities of this new century?

As we examined what was necessary to communicate the myriad challenges in forging a path to greater sustainable use of earth's resources, we began to realize that we were asking students to cope with extraordinarily

complex, challenging, and multifaceted problems for which data can be ambiguous, predictions uncertain, and pathways to greater sustainability counterintuitive. With this realization came the recognition that charting a path toward a sustainable future requires fully self-authored participants who are capable of viewing and applying knowledge in context and who can interpret the perspectives of others in the light of multiple lines of evidence from various disciplines. The challenge became clear: we needed learning goals that not only addressed content and technical skills but also supported growth toward self-authorship; we needed a team of faculty with expertise from a variety of disciplines who were also committed to the concept of making student development a learning goal; and we needed adequate time for learning to occur. This chapter chronicles the process of creating and piloting a core curricular experience that is situated in a learning community, revolves around the theme of sustainability, and provides students with the support necessary to encourage their development toward greater degrees of self-authorship and ultimately effective citizenship.

The Setting: Virginia Tech, a Research 1 University

Undergraduate education and curriculum reform in research institutions is often overlooked and undervalued. The following quote underlines this concern and makes the reform effort noted in this chapter even more significant. "The Association of American Colleges and Universities recently launched a 10-year campaign to 'champion the value of a liberal education' and to 'spark public debate' about just what that is. But the concept may be more alive and well in four-year liberal-arts colleges than it is in our great research universities that are setting the agenda for higher education today. Those institutions are my concern: I fear that undergraduate education in the research university is becoming a project in ruins" (Katz, 2005, p. 1).

An Opportunity for Change. Based on Katz's perspective (2005), Research 1 universities are not the most likely candidates to embrace major curricular experimentation as part of their undergraduate educational mission. Yet while Virginia Tech's leaders have focused on encouraging, facilitating, and developing an ever more ambitious research agenda, they have also recognized the institution's role in educating its twenty-one thousand undergraduates. In 1993, the Center for Excellence in Undergraduate Teaching (CEUT) was established to serve as an "advocate for teaching excellence and for providing various resources and development opportunities for faculty" (Wildman, 2004, p. 247). By the mid-1990s, Virginia Tech had created the Learning Communities Initiative to encourage discussion and implementation of programs that "educated the whole person" (Virginia Tech, 2001, p. 2). It is in this setting that Marcia Baxter Magolda first visited Virginia Tech and began a productive multiyear relationship with faculty that has resulted in the development of several projects founded on student development. The Earth Sustainability project evolved from both enlightening conversations and from ideas generated in a multiyear CEUT-supported faculty study group (Augustine and others, 2002). By May 2003, several faculty members had banded together to put six years of learning and discussion into action.

Development Informing Core Curricular Structure: The Course Series Concept. In May 2003, I (Bekken) invited faculty and graduate students from across disciplines to join in a discussion of how we could cocreate a new undergraduate core curriculum program with the primary goal of structuring the learning environment to encourage development toward self-authorship. Although I was on a mission to create a series of courses that would tackle the theme of sustainability, we recognized that making student development toward self-authorship the primary goal of a restructured general education program allowed for any variety of interdisciplinary themes to emerge as conceptual vehicles that could support this goal. Thus, any emergent curricular structure would have to incorporate the three assumptions of self-authorship theory (Baxter Magolda, 1999): that knowledge is complex and socially constructed, that the self is central to knowledge construction, and that authority and expertise are shared in the mutual construction of knowledge among peers.

Over thirty faculty members responded to the initial workshop discussion, allowing us to shape a structure and define themes of interest around which we could offer pilot programs that responded to our developmental goal. Although many of the faculty members who participated were not directly familiar with self-authorship theory, they were nonetheless intrigued by the concept of a multisemester, integrative learning environment. The vision that emerged from these rich discussions called for us to create multisemester learning communities that would unite faculty with a student cohort over two years during which time each community would investigate an interdisciplinary issue. We dubbed the project Living in the Twenty-First Century and worked together to define themes around which a critical nucleus of faculty would have both creative energy and expertise. By fall 2003, four themes had emerged, each supported by a faculty member coordinator with a unique vision for that theme. But the rigors of breaking new ground are significant, and the demands on faculty do not leave room for much risk taking. By spring 2004, only one theme, Earth Sustainability, had managed to gain approval in the form originally envisioned: a multisemester course series that would satisfy most of the undergraduate core curriculum goals while making development toward self-authorship its foundational goal.

Design and Implementation of the Earth Sustainability Series

The challenge of using resources sustainably is complex and involves choices (who uses, who loses, who decides). Such choices are inherently messy and can be influenced by many stakeholders with differing or competing interests.

NEW DIRECTIONS FOR TEACHING AND LEARNING • DOI: 10.1002/tl

Not uncommonly, both the popular press and introductory textbooks have simplified this complexity to two polarized viewpoints. What is most disturbing about the "debate" approach is that it can give students the false impression that there are only two sides to an issue and that the group drives policies capable of exerting the greater (monetary) influence. This perception is not only incorrect but also leaves students feeling powerless. Therefore, we needed to reframe our approach from a simplistic polarized perspective to a multidisciplinary discussion in which many voices are heard and valued.

We aligned the learning goals to encourage those outcomes essential to grasping the true challenge of sustainability: issues are complex, stakeholders are many and varied, evidence used to inform decisions is provided by many disciplines in which the methods used and assumptions made for gathering it differ, natural and human systems are vast and intricately interconnected, change toward sustainable practice can and does happen when people are empowered, and although there is a lot that we do not yet understand, there is still a lot that we do understand and can act on. For students to begin to develop the multiple perspectives essential to recognizing paths to sustainability so that they can make informed decisions, they must develop the habits of mind and action necessary to weigh evidence in the light of multiple truths and act responsibly as members of a greater global community. In effect, we are asking students to begin charting a path toward effective citizenship, which, according to Baxter Magolda (2004a), requires fully self-authored persons. Thus, sustainability with all of its complexity is an ideal theme in which to encourage development toward self-authorship.

Development Informing the Organization of Content: A Spiraling Curriculum. During the 2003–2004 academic year, a team of faculty and graduate students met weekly to design the Earth Sustainability course series. The design proposal that grew out of this effort not only fulfilled the content and technical skill goals of the core curriculum but also explicitly outlined developmental goals based on Baxter Magolda's self-authorship theory (1999). We selected Bruner's concept of a spiral (1960) as the organizing rubric for building the curriculum. From a content perspective, the spiral provided an organizational structure onto which we could map our investigation of essential resources such as water, energy, earth materials, and food by using a multidisciplinary approach that repeated with each subsequent resource. For example, a resource like fresh water could be examined through several disciplinary windows, such as basic hydrogeology, water cycling, and distribution; economics and water law; water in art, religion, and mythology; climatic variability and its effect on ancient civilizations; ethical questions over the unequal distribution of freshwater resources relative to human populations; and the future availability and management of freshwater resources globally. On completion of the freshwater module, the multidisciplinary approach would be repeated with another resource, such as energy. But the biggest advantage to the curriculum spiral is that it encouraged instructors to develop each new resource with increasing levels

NEW DIRECTIONS FOR TEACHING AND LEARNING • DOI: 10.1002/tl

of intellectual sophistication while promoting increased responsibility for learning. In other words, using a spiraling curriculum model allowed us to unite traditional core curriculum goals—largely content and technical skills—with the goal of explicitly encouraging student development toward self-authorship over four semesters.

But development takes time and cannot be readily affected or discerned over a single semester. Thus, we agreed that the Earth Sustainability series would unfold over several semesters, with a cohort of faculty and students proceeding through it as a single learning community evolving and adjusting with the needs of the participants. Because we could offer the curriculum over two years, we had the freedom to incorporate and ensure the continuity of developmental goals in a way that is not possible with traditional menu-driven general education courses. Table 5.1 lists examples of some of the epistemological, interpersonal, and intrapersonal goals that we are addressing through the multisemester series. These goals link directly to the essential learning outcomes advocated by various educational research organizations and policy centers (Association of American Colleges and Universities, 2002, 2005; Ratcliff, Johnson, and Gaff, 2004; National Center for Public Policy and Higher Education, 2004; American Association for Higher Education, American College Personnel Association, and National Association of Student Personnel Administrators, 1998; Willimon and Naylor, 1995; American Association for the Advancement of Science, 1989). They also are rarely directly or explicitly addressed in general education.

Development Informing Pedagogy: The Learning Partnerships Model. In our quest to offer the Earth Sustainability core course series, we had successfully moved beyond the traditional content-focused design by making the journey toward self-authorship a major learning goal. Our next challenge was to develop pedagogies to support this foundational goal. Baxter Magolda (2004b) articulates a model: a learning partnership, through which the goal of encouraging students to journey toward self-authorship can be realized. The Learning Partnerships Model (LPM) is founded on three principles by which faculty support students during their journey: (1) validate each student's capacity to know, (2) situate learning in the student's experience, and (3) create a partnership in which the participants mutually construct meaning (Baxter Magolda, 2004b). In effect, the pedagogical design of assignments, class meetings, and out-of-class activities must both support and challenge students by valuing their experience and learning skills but also by providing them with the impetus and support to progress to more complex, comprehensive, and adequate modes of learning and thinking. Thus, the learning goals, content, and pedagogy must concomitantly reassure students yet express high expectations of their becoming increasingly responsible for their learning.

Development Informing Faculty: The Faculty Development Seminar. Introducing new ways of teaching and learning into the curriculum is difficult given the lack of attention to preparing new professors to be teachers.

Table 5.1. Examples of Developmental Learning Goals for the Four Semesters of the Earth Sustainability Project

	Content and Development Themes			
	Semester 1— Worldviews and Water: Addressing Complexity	*Semester 2— Energy and Shelter: Recognizing Assumptions and Arguments*	*Semester 3— Food and Agriculture: Making Connections*	*Semester 4— Waste, Health, and Pathways to the Future: Responsibility and Empowerment*
Epistemological developmental goals				
Information literacy	• Access, retrieve, and cite information using library catalogue • Construct keyword searches	• Evaluate and cite Web-based resources • Use databases for article searches • Annotate and cite	• Access information sources not archived in the library or on the Internet • Cite sources in appropriate format	• Extract, annotate, and cite information from technical databases • Evaluate information sources
Reading to learn	• Develop targeted reading skills: texts, fiction narratives	• Develop targeted reading skills: nonfiction narratives	• Develop targeted reading skills: scientific, technical	• Use targeted reading skills in all genres to seek evidence
Developing a research process	• Complete one qualitative and one quantitative natural science project or report	• Complete one qualitative and one quantitative social science project or report	• Construct one qualitative and one quantitative natural science project or report	• Construct one qualitative and one quantitative social science project or report
Selecting research methods	• Recognize the link between methods and evidence in creating disciplinary knowledge	• Collect evidence • Identify and use discipline-specific methods	• Characterize similarities and differences in methods between disciplines	• Discern appropriate methodologies based on outcomes and evidence in knowledge creation

Using assumptions and arguments	• Sort opinions from arguments supported by evidence • Classify arguments	• Identify assumptions • Discover disciplinary biases • Recognize complexity	• Evaluate arguments and supporting assumptions • Challenge disciplinary bias	• Frame arguments from multiple perspectives, justify assumptions, assess evidence
Intentional learning: Reading and note taking	• Use reading guides • Develop note-taking strategies: outlines, concept maps, matrix	• Use reading prompts • Practice and post verbal and written notes using each strategy	• Create and discuss reading prompts • Record and post notes using all strategies	• Create and discuss reading prompts • Choose note-taking strategy and post
Interpersonal developmental goals				
Developing dialogue	• Describe and model active listening • Recognize value of diverse opinions	• Describe and model constructive dialogue • Identify personal assumptions and biases	• Practice dialogue with diverse others • Reserve judgment	• Engage in dialogue with peers • Value difference as a learning opportunity
Working in groups and teams	• Practice setting group norms, goals, tasks, and timetables	• Practice consensus-building techniques • Improve reliability	• With guidance, plan and complete a group project with product	• Independently plan and complete a group project with product
Intrapersonal developmental goals				
Developing voice	• Recognize personal positions and perspectives • Keep a written log	• Discover and describe basis for perspective • Continue written log	• Reflect on changed perspectives by evaluating journal	• Describe a process for self-reflection and self-evaluation
Developing agency	• Describe personal goals, articulate plan	• Assess and align goals and behaviors	• Reassess and align goals with behaviors	• Describe process of alignment and agency

NEW DIRECTIONS FOR TEACHING AND LEARNING • DOI: 10.1002/tl

Although subject content is the focus of their education, the pedagogy of teaching is not. "Professors are rarely exposed to research on teaching during graduate school. . . . Freshly minted PhDs typically teach the way their favorite professors taught. This pattern introduces a strong conservative bias into college instruction, a bias reinforced by the tendency of many faculties to regard the choice of teaching methods as the exclusive prerogative of individual professors rather than a fit subject for collective deliberation" (Bok, 2006, p. 2)

If an evolutionary bridge (Kegan, 1994) is needed to connect students to new ways of thinking, then it is equally necessary to connect faculty to new models for teaching and learning. While we could argue that in the first term of the Earth Sustainability series, it might be appropriate to begin with a moderately traditional classroom setting, because that is familiar to students' experience, it is equally appropriate to begin to shift toward a partnership in which authority is shared within a learning community. To support us in implementing pedagogies consistent with the LPM, Terry Wildman, a cognitive psychologist and director of CEUT, organized an ongoing bimonthly faculty seminar to both inform and transform our practice. Shelli Fowler, director of the Graduate Education Development Institute, an English professor, and an expert on learning communities, is a regular advisor in the seminar series. Baxter Magolda also has joined us once each term to observe, reflect, and advise us on our progress toward creating an effective integrative learning community and a learning partnership. These contributors have been invaluable in their knowledge, support, and encouragement of the project, but we have found that daily discussions with members of our own team of instructional faculty have provided us with many of the tools that are necessary to build the faculty developmental bridges essential to our unique interpretation and implementation of the LPM for this learning community. We have come to appreciate that the model is dynamic and that it must be uniquely tailored to the needs and strengths of each community.

Development Informing the Institution: Structural Challenges. In March 2004, the provost of Virginia Tech sent a letter to faculty encouraging them to "review, refine, revitalize, resource, and reward activities" that support a "more fully integrated core" curriculum. He called for the "removal of barriers" so that a culture of innovation and creativity in core curricula could be fostered. While these efforts have prompted a dialogue over the future of Virginia Tech's core curriculum, the reality is that "educational decisions made decades ago are now institutionalized in physical and bureaucratic structures and continue to exert tremendous influence over what is possible" (Wildman, 2004, p. 251). How, then, does one proceed?

As we designed the Earth Sustainability course series, we began to understand and embrace our own unique institutional history and structure and accept that these institutionalized physical and bureaucratic structures could provide a foundation from which a new program would evolve. With this realization, we situated our project within the goals of Virginia Tech's core curriculum and the constraints of the governance process. Thus, our learning goals for the Earth Sustainability course series incorporate Virginia Tech's rich set of content and technical core goals, recognizing that the process of working toward extant learning goals must be founded in and grounded by a clear appreciation of student development.

In an analogous manner, providing adequate credit to faculty who work as a team does not fit with Virginia Tech's method of assigning a single full-time-equivalent faculty member to a course. As the pilot series began in the fall of 2004, we had become a community of scholars, and we shared a common vision for the overarching goal of encouraging student development toward self-authorship. This goal necessitated faculty continuity. Thus, we rejected the division-of-labor model (one faculty per course) in lieu of a collaborative teamwork model in which the principal instructors would attend as many of the class meetings as possible and share in assignment design and evaluation. This required that the university develop an alternative model for assigning faculty teaching loads. As a result, an alternative way to account for collaborative faculty effort is under development.

Regardless of theme, the course series concept is integrative and interdisciplinary. It must draw on expertise from many colleges, and therefore housing it at the university level is appropriate. We created a new designator, the university core course series, with fervent hope that other themes would emerge over time. To encourage participation by all colleges, full student credit hours are assigned to each department that loans faculty to the project. To encourage faculty participation, we began piloting a teaching sabbatical program began in fall 2006 in which departments receive two years of buy-behind support for loaning faculty to the project. And finally, to oversee and support this project, as well as others that are undergoing similar research and development, the new Center for Undergraduate Education was created in January 2006. Thus, we are becoming confident that the barriers to innovation are being surmounted as the course series concept demonstrates success toward its learning goals.

Evaluation of the Earth Sustainability Course Series

In Research 1 institutions, recognition of scholarship is conferred through the acquisition of sponsored research, peer-reviewed publications in scholarly journals or books, and awards. Rarely have projects involving the core curriculum ventured into this competitive arena. Yet this is one of the powerful frames in which success is judged and institutional support awarded. Therefore, it became essential that we create a thorough evaluation plan, not only for our own edification and that of the university but also for the extrinsic value placed on any project that has successfully received sponsored research support at the national level. The details of that assessment and evaluation project are beyond the scope of this chapter, and the data for the pilot are still being collected; however, we have watched students change and can provide snapshots of what we have observed in the

NEW DIRECTIONS FOR TEACHING AND LEARNING • DOI: 10.1002/tl

classroom and through their stories that began with their first week of classes as freshmen (August 2004) and have continued with snapshots added at the end of their first (December 2004), second (May 2005), and third terms (December 2005).

Selecting the Earth Sustainability Pilot and Control Groups. During summer orientation 2004, fifty incoming first-year students were recruited from five of the seven colleges that serve undergraduate students at Virginia Tech. Of these fifty, twenty-three students enrolled in the Earth Sustainability course series. The remainder could not enroll due to scheduling conflicts, but twenty of these students agreed to participate in a control group. We are currently in the fourth and final semester, with nineteen students remaining in the Earth Sustainability series and twelve remaining from the original control group, with eight additional students recruited to replace those who opted not to continue with the study. Because the number of students involved in this initial phase is small, we are conducting a multimethod, in-depth assessment that will evaluate gains in epistemological development, critical thinking, scientific reasoning, student engagement in learning, and inter- and intrapersonal development. This study will provide preliminary evidence by which we can compare gains made in the integrative course series core model with the traditional menu-driven general education model. Furthermore, by evaluating this phase in depth with a smaller group of students, we can test existing measures and develop additional measures that we are applying to the expanded Earth Sustainability series, which began in August 2006, and to other thematic course series as they are designed and piloted.

Observations of the Phase 1 Earth Sustainability Cohort. As we write this chapter, we are finishing the fourth and final semester of the Earth Sustainability pilot. Of the nineteen remaining students out of the twenty-three who self-selected into the course series at the beginning of fall 2004, five are male and fourteen female, thirteen are from Virginia and six out of state, and fourteen are from metropolitan areas and five from rural communities. The majority of students come from middle-income and working-class families. There were no African Americans in the group and no foreign students. Three of the students are Asian American (Vietnam, Japan, and Korea), and one is Hispanic (Costa Rica). The remaining students are Caucasian. Most students have jobs on campus to help defray costs, and at least two are completely independent of their families and are self-supporting. Six had not declared majors at the beginning of the series, but all had declared a major preference after the first term. Of the seven colleges that serve undergraduate students, student majors represent five colleges. By major, seven students are majoring in natural or applied sciences, nine in social sciences, and three in humanities.

Although over forty faculty members will have been involved with the course series in some capacity during the initial design phase and two-year pilot offering, two faculty coordinators—a humanist and a scientist—and one graduate teaching assistant have designed, organized, and implemented the four Earth Sustainability courses. Two other faculty members, another scientist and a librarian, were significantly involved in the design and implementation of select course themes (food) or objectives (information literacy). Two English instructors modified and taught the English sections dedicated to this pilot effort. In addition, over thirty disciplinary faculty members will have visited the classroom to provide guest lectures, participate in class discussions, or offer laboratory, field, or workshop modules. More than one student has remarked on the incredible opportunity to meet faculty and learn about other disciplines from all over campus.

Changes in Student Perceptions During the First Term At the beginning of fall semester 2004, we gave students two exercises: one in which they were asked to define the term *sustainability* and state what they wanted to see sustained and the second in which they were asked to envision the future based on four worldview-driven stories of what it might look like (Costanza, 2000) These two short written exercises allowed us to simultaneously assess students' knowledge base and epistemological development. We found that of the twenty-three students who began the series, only three suggested that charting a path toward sustainability was not simple and straightforward. Nineteen of the students responded to this task as absolute knowers (Baxter Magolda, 1992) and indicated that issues in sustainable use could be solved if people would cooperate, there would not be a problem if so many humans were not so greedy or our culture were not so focused on technology, and the government needs to do something to fix the problem. These responses reveal the knowledge assumptions of absolute knowers: answers exist, these answers have rights and wrongs, authority figures know the answers, and authority figures need to take action and do the right thing. One student did not address the issue at all.

At the end of the term, we asked students to review each of four assignments that had dealt with issues of complexity and authority, including the two introductory assignments described, and reflect on their changed perspectives. Approximately half of the students rejected the theses of their first two essays, finding them to be naive or simplistic, while the rest of the students held to the theses expressed in their original essays, even though most indicated that they would now add greater depth and detail to their descriptions. Several students voiced a desire to create their own visions for the future rather than adapt any from the source that we had provided to them. Three students indicated that they had become quite involved with the fourth assignment, researching ideas and finding outside sources well beyond the intent of the activity.

More than any other single assignment during the first term, this reflection gave us direct insight into how the students had perceived themselves when the term began and how their perspectives had changed. Most essay reflections provided not only a snapshot of their epistemological development but also their interpersonal and intrapersonal development in ways that we had not anticipated. We found this window into development so enlightening that we were motivated to focus the learning objectives of select assignments and activities around developmental subthemes for each of the three subsequent semesters. We chose three epistemological subthemes, one for each semester: recognizing assumptions and arguments, making connections, and taking responsibility/becoming empowered (Table 5.1).

Changes in Student Perception at the End of Second Term. In the second term, we examined resources that provide energy and shelter using the multidisciplinary, multiperspective approach described for the first term. The epistemological subtheme that we had selected to support the developmental goals for this term focused on understanding empirical methods, methodological assumptions, and forms of argument. As we began the term, we knew that many of the students had strongly held beliefs about truth. Several accepted scientific truths, a few accepted religious truths, and many accepted as truth the arguments of their preferred political parties or their parents or both. To help them avoid descending into simple polemics on issues such as the age of the earth, evolution, or oil drilling in Alaska, we incorporated several short in-class exercises and targeted discussions that provided them with tools to listen to one another while reserving judgment.

Near the end of the term, we asked students to reflect on their ability to listen thoughtfully, recognize assumptions, and expose or create arguments by reviewing three of their papers in which several of these skills had been addressed directly or indirectly. All but two students commented explicitly that their ability to listen while reserving judgment had increased. Fifteen students wrote that on most issues discussed in the first two exercises, they did not change position or perspective but had discovered that they could be more open and less defensive when discussing sensitive issues. Two students admitted to changing perspectives entirely.

It was far more challenging for students to assess their ability to uncover assumptions and recognize arguments, whether their own or others. Only eleven of the twenty students who had continued after first term addressed this theme directly in their reflections, and of those, only seven demonstrated that they could identify an assumption and distinguish it from a knowledge claim.

Using the descriptions of the four domains of Baxter Magolda's epistemological reflection model (1992) to review the end-of-term reflection, we estimate that up to twelve students are still relying on external formulas for guidance; however, only five of these students appeared to retain largely absolutist constructions of the world around them as compared with fifteen of the original twenty-three who had been enrolled during first term.

Changes in Student Perception at the End of Third Term. During the third term, we examined food and agricultural resources, again using a multidisciplinary curriculum spiral, but we also asked that students commit to a service-learning project through which they could become more familiar with the local food-producing community in southwest Virginia. The subtheme for this third course focused on making connections. The students were now sophomores, and nineteen of the original twenty-three were still enrolled. As sophomores, several of the assignment products such as lab reports, persuasive essays, or annotated bibliographies were no longer completely new to them, nor were the empirical methods used to investigate the topics. As a result, we wanted to evaluate to what degree these habits of mind were becoming habituated—hence, the idea of asking students to reflect on the subtheme of connections in their end-of-term reflections.

Newell and Davis (1988) and Davis and Newell (1981) describe the ability of students in interdisciplinary programs to make conceptual connections and transfer both process and content knowledge between subjects far more adeptly than their peers. The reflections from this term clearly support this claim, with fifteen of the nineteen students making at least three significant connections between what they had learned in the course and their personal, campus, or future lives. Seven of these students described how empowered they felt as a result of the knowledge that they had gained. Eighteen of the students wrote with authenticity in a voice that was not evident at the end of second semester. One student missed the point of the assignment so could not be evaluated. Overall, students' comments described an evolving sense of identity, interconnectedness, and empowerment.

Conclusions and Future Work

What we have seen during the nearly four semesters of the Earth Sustainability pilot is a remarkable transformation in student development as evidenced by four snapshots of written reflective work over time that capture how the students conceptualize complexity and authority, whether they recognize fundamental assumptions and arguments, and how they apply or transfer disciplinary knowledge beyond disciplinary boundaries. The perspectives they offered in their reflective essays suggest that the majority entered the university as absolute or dualistic knowers with a reliance on external formulas, but they rapidly began to evolve to far more complex and incipiently self-authored ways of knowing by the end of the third semester. We have witnessed (1) gains in the precision and clarity of writing, speaking, and thinking; (2) an increasing ability to recognize assumptions and arguments; (3) increased sensitivity to ethical issues; (4) the connection to and integration of content and skills into personal, campus, and family life; (5) enlarged perspectives; (6) increased listening skills; (7) a tolerance for ambiguity; and (8) a sensitivity to bias. Although we hypothesize that the rate of this developmental change is more dramatic for students within the Earth Sustainability series than for those in a traditional general education core, we cannot yet make this claim, as the comparative research study for both Earth Sustainability and control student groups is still in progress. Both groups will be evaluated annually through their senior year, by which time the control students also will have completed their core requirements.

In fall 2006, we offered an expanded version of the Earth Sustainability series to seventy-five incoming first-year students. We plan to evaluate the intellectual development of students in both the second expanded phase of Earth Sustainability and a complementary control group over four years as well. Evidence from both studies will shed light on the degree to which making student intellectual development a primary learning goal of core curricula achieves the desired learning outcomes that have been advocated by many influential educational specialists and organizations for over twenty years (Association of American Colleges and Universities, 2002, 2005; Ratcliff, Johnson and Gaff, 2004; National Center for Public Policy and Higher Education, 2004; American Association for Higher Education, American College Personnel Association, and National Association of Student Personnel Administrators, 1998; Willimon and Naylor, 1995; American Association for the Advancement of Science, 1989).

Acknowledgments

This project is a group effort and would not have been possible without the talent, support, and commitment of our Virginia Tech colleagues in the Earth Sustainability Group: Carola Haas (Fisheries and Wildlife Sciences), Margaret Merrill (University Libraries), Lisa Norris (English), Barbara Reeves (Interdisciplinary Studies, Science and Technology in Society, and History), and Tiffany Trent (English). In addition, over thirty Virginia Tech faculty members have contributed to the curricular design and initial offering of the project. Insightful comments, suggestions, and feedback about student development were also provided by Shelli Fowler (Graduate Education Development Institute), Marcia Baxter Magolda (Department of Educational Leadership, Miami of Ohio), Deborah Olsen (Department of Higher Education), and Terry Wildman (Center for Excellence in Undergraduate Teaching). A grant from the National Science Foundation (DUE-0536694 to Deborah Olsen and Barbara Bekken) and Virginia Tech's Office of Institutional Research are supporting acquisition of data on student learning and development. Additional support for this project has been provided by Virginia Tech's Center for Excellence in Undergraduate Teaching, the Provost's Office, the Graduate School, Virginia Tech Libraries, and the Departments of Geosciences, Fisheries and Wildlife Sciences, and Interdisciplinary Studies.

References

American Association for Higher Education, American College Personnel Association, and National Association of Student Personnel Administrators. *Powerful Partnerships: A Shared Responsibility for Learning.* Washington, D.C.: American Association for Higher Education, American College Personnel Association, and National Association for Student Personnel Administrators, 1998.

American Association for the Advancement of Science. *Science for All Americans: Project 2061.* New York: Oxford University Press, 1989.

Association of American Colleges and Universities. *Greater Expectations: A New Vision of Learning as a Nation Goes to College.* Washington, D.C.: Association of American Colleges and Universities, 2002.

Association of American Colleges and Universities. *Peer Review: Emerging Trends and Key Debates in Undergraduate Education.* Washington, D.C.: Association of American Colleges and Universities, 2005.

Augustine, D., and others. "What Is a Feminist Pedagogy for the Sciences?" *Virginia Tech's Center for Excellence in Undergraduate Teaching Newsletter,* Spring 2002, pp. 17–19.

Baxter Magolda, M. B. *Knowing and Reasoning in College: Gender-Related Patterns in Students' Intellectual Development.* San Francisco: Jossey-Bass, 1992.

Baxter Magolda, M. B. *Creating Contexts for Learning and Self-Authorship.* Nashville, Tenn.: Vanderbilt University Press, 1999.

Baxter Magolda, M. B. *Making Their Own Way: Narratives for Transforming Higher Education to Promote Self-Authorship.* Sterling, Va.: Stylus Publishing, 2001.

Baxter Magolda, M. B. "Self-Authorship as the Common Goal of 21st-Century Education." In M. B. Baxter Magolda and P. M. King (eds.), *Learning Partnerships.* Sterling, Va.: Stylus, 2004a.

Baxter Magolda, M. B. "Learning Partnerships Model: A Framework for Promoting Self-Authorship." In M. B. Baxter Magolda and P. M. King (eds.), *Learning Partnerships.* Sterling, Va.: Stylus, 2004b.

Bok, D. *Our Underachieving Colleges.* Princeton, N.J.: Princeton University Press, 2006.

Bruner, J. *The Process of Education.* Cambridge, Mass.: Harvard University Press, 1960.

Costanza, R. "Visions of Alternative (Unpredictable) Futures and Their Use in Policy Analysis." *Conservation Ecology,* 2000, *4*(1), 5. Retrieved May 31, 2006, from http://www.consecol.org/vol4/iss1/art5.

Davis, A., and Newell, W. "Those Experimental Colleges of the 1960s: Where Are They Now That We Need Them?" *Chronicle of Higher Education,* Nov. 18, 1981, p. 64.

Katz, S. N. "Liberal Education on the Rope." *Chronicle Review, Chronicle of Higher Education,* Apr. 1, 2005, *51*(30), B6. Retrieved May 31, 2006, from http://chronicle.com/weekly/v51/i30/30b00601.htm.

Kegan, R. *In over Our Heads: The Mental Demand of Modern Life.* Cambridge, Mass.: Harvard University Press, 1994.

National Center for Public Policy and Higher Education. *Measuring Up: The National Report Card on Higher Education.* San Jose, Calif.: National Center for Public Policy and Higher Education, 2004.

Newell, W., and Davis, A., "Education for Citizenship: The Role of Progressive Education and Interdisciplinary Studies." *Innovative Higher Education,* 1988, *13*(1), 27–37.

Ratcliff, J. L., Johnson, D. K., and Gaff, J. G. "Changing the General Education Curriculum." New Directions for Higher Education, no. 125. San Francisco: Jossey-Bass, 2004.

Virginia Tech. "Virginia Tech Vision Statement." 2001. Retrieved May 31, 2006, from http://www.unirel.vt.edu/vt/mission.html.

Wildman, T. M. "The Learning Partnerships Model: Framing Institutional and Faculty Development." In M. B. Baxter Magolda and P. M. King, P. M. (eds.), *Learning Partnerships.* Sterling, Va.: Stylus, 2004.

Willimon, W. H., and Naylor, T. H. *The Abandoned Generation: Rethinking Higher Education.* Grand Rapids, Mich.: Eerdmans, 1995.

BARBARA BEKKEN *is an assistant professor of geology in the Department of Geosciences at Virginia Polytechnic Institute and State University in Blacksburg, Virginia, and director of the Living in the 21st Century Integrative Studies Program and the Earth Sustainability Pilot Project.*

JOAN MARIE *is a doctoral candidate in the Department of Science and Technology in Society at Virginia Polytechnic Institute and State University in Blacksburg, Virginia, and coordinator of the Earth Sustainability series.*

6

Innovative educational practice reveals the secrets to enabling complex learning and self-authorship.

Self-Authorship: The Foundation for Twenty-First-Century Education

Marcia B. Baxter Magolda

Educators, legislators, and the American public concur that learning outcomes of higher education should include effective citizenship, critical thinking and complex problem solving, interdependent relations with diverse others, and mature decision making. Many students enter college having learned how to follow formulas for success, lacking exposure to diverse perspectives, and unclear about their own beliefs, identities, and values (Baxter Magolda, 2001b). Moving from these entering characteristics to intended learning outcomes requires transformational learning, or "how we learn to negotiate and act on our own purposes, values, feelings, and meanings rather than those we have uncritically assimilated from others" (Mezirow, 2000, p. 8). Extracting themselves from what they have uncritically assimilated from authorities to define their own purposes, values, feelings, and meanings involves far more than information and skill acquisition. It requires a transformation of their views of knowledge, their identity, and their relations with others. Twenty-first-century learning outcomes require self-authorship: the internal capacity to define one's belief system, identity, and relationships (Baxter Magolda, 2001b; Kegan, 1994).

The preceding chapters emphasize the importance of integrating what we know about learning, development, and educational practice. We know that complex learning outcomes require developing internal belief systems constructed through critical analysis of multiple perspectives. We also know that developing internal belief systems is interwoven with developing

internal values that shape our identities and relations with others. Thus, self-authorship forms a developmental foundation for advanced learning outcomes. We also know that many college environments do not offer learners sufficient guidance to develop these internal systems, and thus learners rely on external formulas for decisions about beliefs and values. Research has identified models of practice, particularly the Learning Partnerships Model (LPM; Baxter Magolda, 2004a), to guide educational practice in linking learning and development toward self-authorship. Assessment research is advancing our ability to identify students' development for the purpose of guiding practice and judging its effectiveness.

In this chapter, I merge previous chapters in this volume with additional research and practice to highlight theoretical advances in linking self-authorship and twenty-first-century learning outcomes, innovative practice to promote self-authorship and twenty-first-century learning outcomes, and research in progress to refine and assess the relationship of self-authorship and learning outcomes.

Theoretical Advances in Linking Self-Authorship and Learning Outcomes

Nowhere are the links between self-authorship and college learning outcomes clearer than in the stories of college graduates who are now managing their adult lives. Participants in my twenty-year longitudinal study of young adult development and learning (Baxter Magolda, 2001b) convey that college learning focused on knowledge and intellect is insufficient for mature adult functioning. Gavin, one of the students in my study, reported, "It's a lot more emotional learning once you get out [of college] because before you always knew you could always just give up and go home. Now you can't give up and you can't go home" (Baxter Magolda, 2001b, p. 285). Mark explained the difference similarly: "In the college classroom there is a focus on intellect and not necessarily the feel of what is going on. It is a much more controlled environment. What you learn after college is how out of control the environment is. Life is about dealing with those particular out-of-control situations" (year 19 interview).

Mark's insight about "out-of-control situations" reflects the complexity these young adults faced daily in their postcollege lives. Whether it was a lawyer winning a legal case, a doctor making wise treatment decisions, a teacher or social worker making decisions about a child's future, a businessperson making significant financial decisions, a parent comforting an infant, or a partner trying to understand how to function in a mutual relationship, complexity was the mainstay of their adult lives.

Dawn articulated more specifically what this "feel" or "emotional learning" involved and how it incorporated knowledge and intellect. At age thirty-seven, she described succeeding in her professional and personal life on the basis of wisdom:

NEW DIRECTIONS FOR TEACHING AND LEARNING • DOI: 10.1002/tl

It's starting to feel—more like wisdom than knowledge. To me knowledge is an awareness of when you know things. You know them as facts; they are there in front of you. When you possess the wisdom, you've lived those facts, that information so fully that it takes on a whole different aspect than just knowing. It is like you absorbed that information into your entire being. Not just that you know things. It is something deeper. Knowledge is brain—wisdom comes from a different place I feel like. Something deeper connecting with your brain so that you have something different to draw from. A point where knowing you are going to do something—the knowledge has a deeper level—internal, intuitive, centered in entire being, the essential part of you that just—makes the basic knowledge pale by comparison [year 19 interview].

This inner wisdom, as Dawn called it, combined knowledge with internally derived beliefs, values, emotions, and identity. Mark expressed this combination: "Just because intellect points you in a particular direction doesn't mean that is the right direction. More enduring values are grounded in love, trust, faith. Intellectual calculus may lead you to devalue those things" (year 19 interview). Mark, Dawn, and their peers portrayed their professional decision making as stemming from this internal wisdom. They had come to live the knowledge base of their respective fields, merging it with their internal sense of themselves and their social relations.

Complexity in professional life was accompanied by complexity in personal life. Dawn described how inner wisdom helped her understand and work with having multiple sclerosis:

For the first three years, I've had to be a warrior—that has been my process with the MS thing. Strong, bold, brave, conquer to keep myself going forward. Somewhere in all of that I realized that I could let go of warrior, I'm steady, moving forward, now I kind of feel like my MS is more of a friend that helps guide me, give me information on how to best proceed on my path. A shift in 'okay, I have MS' and I'm going to work with it, it with me, we have a great partnership together. My life has gotten much easier. I know how hard to push myself, know when to say stop [year 19 interview].

Dawn's ability to define her beliefs and values internally, a process she articulated over the course of her late twenties and early thirties, helped her frame what MS meant in her life. Other longitudinal participants used this self-authored inner wisdom to make meaning of personal or familial physical and mental health challenges, loss of loved ones, and a variety of stressful experiences such as a spouse serving in Iraq.

Another layer of complexity for my longitudinal participants came in relationships with family and partners. Building and maintaining mature, interdependent relationships with others while constructing an internal belief system and sense of self required a delicate balance of self and other. Mark offered this example:

There is a point where spouses have to allow the other one individuality. I respect that position and won't interfere with you following it, but I have my own track. If it is a life of love and respect that you are going for, those things have to be minimized. Listen to perspective, come to understand opinion, then there is a mutual respect to allow the other spouse to not go with it. Come to mutual agreement to respect one another's choices [year 19 interview].

Mark emphasized mutual respect as the key to good relationships. Dawn clarified that self-respect stands at the core of this ability when she said, "If you respect yourself, it is pretty much a given that you will respect others. Treating others with compassion and understanding can only happen when you've achieved a certain level of that yourself" (Baxter Magolda, 2004b, p. 20). These perspectives demonstrate that self-authorship of identity, relationships, and knowledge are necessary for mature adult decision making, interdependent relationships, and effective citizenship.

Some students encounter these complexities in the college environment, if not earlier. Those who have been marginalized due to race, ethnicity, social class, gender, or sexual orientation encounter what Jane Pizzolato (2005) calls provocative experiences as they pursue college goals. Students with low privilege sometimes developed their own internal goals contrary to family and cultural expectations in order to pursue college (Pizzolato, 2003). Many were able to solidify their self-authored visions of themselves despite discrimination in the college environment (Pizzolato, 2004). Similarly, self-authored adult learners in an English as a Second Language program were able to critique and reject discriminatory cultural messages in their community college environment because they evaluated these messages on the basis of their internal standards and values (Helsing, Broderick, and Hammerman, 2001). Lesbian college students who were developing self-authorship were better able to decide internally how external contexts influenced their identities (Abes and Jones, 2004). Movement toward self-authorship, particularly in the cognitive dimension, helped Latina college students construct more positive ethnic identities (Torres and Baxter Magolda, 2004).

Many students, however, do not encounter these complexities during college and make important decisions through reliance on external authority. Anne Laughlin and Elizabeth Creamer's research in Chapter Four advances understanding of the earlier phases of the journey toward self-authorship. By using mixed methods and carefully holding multiple possibilities together during analysis of data from 117 college women, Laughlin and Creamer illuminate the intricacies of decision making that appears to be self-authored but is not. Their analysis revealed that consulting with others did not necessarily mean considering multiple perspectives, that confidence to make decisions independently was more likely tied to commitment to unexamined choices rather than an internally generated set of criteria, and that one's relationship with an authority figure was more important than the person's own expertise in decision making. These findings emphasize that why college women listen to or ignore authorities' advice, why they are confident, and how they regard authorities determine the extent of their self-authorship rather than the act of consulting others or expressing confidence. These nuances are important for theoretically refining the concept of self-authorship as well as for assessing it effectively.

Collectively, this research illustrates that introducing college students to complexity and enabling them to deal with it meaningfully promotes self-authorship. Thus, college is a prime context in which to introduce provocative experiences, portray accurately the complexity of adult life, and guide students through the developmental transformations that lead toward inner wisdom. Innovations in educational practice offer hope that promoting self-authorship during college is a realistic goal.

Innovations in Educational Practice

My longitudinal participants' stories from college, graduate and professional school, diverse employment contexts, and personal lives yielded the dynamics that introduce complexity and promote self-authorship in intellectual, identity and relational development. The resulting LPM (Baxter Magolda, 2004a), already described in this volume, is guiding innovative practice with promising results.

Curricular and Pedagogical Innovations. Virginia Tech's Earth Sustainability multisemester course series that Barbara Bekken and Joan Marie described in Chapter Five is organized using the LPM to achieve the foundational goal of self-authorship. Their organization of learning goals in a developmental sequence coupled with learning partnership pedagogy yielded progress on learning goals and self-authorship. The authors observed increased sophistication in thinking, speaking, and writing; recognizing assumptions, bias, and arguments; openness to larger perspectives; tolerance for ambiguity; and translation of learning to personal life. These outcomes were accompanied by increased development of internal voice, beliefs, and values. These data are particularly exciting because the students in Earth Sustainability took the courses in their first two years of college.

Miami University's School of Interdisciplinary Studies (SIS) used the LPM to develop a four-year writing curriculum to enable students to complete their interdisciplinary theses. Organized around the developmental journey toward self-authorship, the curriculum "helps students progress steadily through three phases, from engagement with expressive modes to an increasingly critical awareness of and proficiency in disciplinary forms to interdisciplinary scholarship" (Haynes, 2004, p. 65). Learning goals increase in complexity each semester, gradually introducing the complexity required for self-authorship. Support from the LPM pedagogy resulted in senior theses that reflected creation of new knowledge, comparison of assumptions from multiple disciplines, and understanding of the insights and limitations of particular perspectives or lines of thought.

Encouraged by the learning outcomes gains and thesis success in the SIS writing curriculum, Haynes undertook a reinvention of the university honors program in which students were also struggling with the senior thesis. She and her staff chose the motto "Scholarship, leadership, and service" to integrate the epistemological, intrapersonal, and interpersonal dimensions of development (Haynes, 2006). The curriculum offers a gradual progression from exposure to college-level scholarship in the first year, to deeper engagement in scholarship in the middle years, to building a lifelong commitment to scholarship in the senior year. The cocurriculum offers a gradual progression from identification of values and exposure to diverse others in the first year, to refining values and learning to work effectively with diverse others in the middle years, to reflecting on one's role as a global citizen and making life plans in the senior year. Increased collaboration among all involved in the honors program, from admission staff to faculty to residence hall staff, and grounded in the LPM provides a consistent balance of challenge and support for dealing with complexity. The results after five years are remarkable. Haynes reported that the high quality of student work, evident in faculty judgments and external awards, is likely related to the quadrupling of faculty volunteering to participate in honors teaching and advising. Students, including students of color, first-generation college students, and diverse socioeconomic-status students, are flocking to the program despite the doubling of curricular requirements and addition of cocurricular requirements. The retention rate has more than doubled, and even with a substantial increase in course offerings, courses are at capacity. Haynes concluded that students seek out rigorous learning opportunities when those opportunities offer holistic development.

The goals of Casa de la Solidaridad, a one-semester immersion experience in El Salvador, resonate with the twenty-first-century learning goals of most college programs. Casa goals include students' expanding their imaginations and ability to think critically and contextually and becoming global citizens who act consistently with their own beliefs and values, "to become, each in their own way, collaborators in promoting global solidarity" (Yonkers-Talz, 2004, p. 151). The Casa curriculum, pedagogy, field experience in the local community, living-learning community including University of Central America students, and purposeful focus on reflection are all explicitly grounded in the LPM. Complexity is inherent in the immersion in an impoverished country and relationships with diverse others. The supportive components of the LPM are crucial to help students maximize learning from encounters with complexity. Kevin Yonkers-Talz, codirector of the Casa, follows the Casa participants longitudinally to assess the effectiveness of the program. In the six years since the Casa began, he has observed that it is typical of participants to think critically and contextually about poverty, international policy, and their own role in the world as a result of the program. The powerful stories participants share reveal that they engage big questions about their internal beliefs, values, purposes, and relations with others (Yonkers-Talz, 2004).

Many colleges endorse the Casa's learning outcome of developing intercultural maturity. Helping undergraduates achieve this outcome is challenging because intercultural maturity requires a self-authored identity able to engage with diverse others without fear of disapproval (Kegan, 1994; King and Baxter Magolda, 2005). Using the Framework of Multicultural Education (which lays out increasingly complex cognitive goals leading to multicultural outcomes and self-authorship) in conjunction with the LPM in a business course, Anne Hornak and Anna Ortiz (2004) provide evidence that breakthroughs are possible. They structured this semester-length course around five increasingly complex steps: understanding culture, learning about other cultures, recognizing and deconstructing white culture, recognizing the legitimacy of other cultures, and developing a multicultural outlook. The LPM support principles of welcoming students' experience and perspectives and engaging in mutual exploration opened students' minds to the influences of their pasts, how culture is created, and engendered responsibility for learning about other cultures. Students struggled to own white privilege, in part due to lack of exposure to diversity and understanding how it affected their lives. The growth that students reported in the course support the notion that a longer-term curriculum of sequenced challenges similar to those Haynes's and Bekken's teams have developed would be useful in helping students achieve intercultural maturity.

Intercultural maturity is one of the goals of the Urban Leadership Internship Program (ULIP) housed in Miami's honors and scholars program. This ten-week course, followed by a ten-week summer internship, aims to help students define their vocational goals, achieve a deeper understanding of themselves, and explore urban environments. Designed using the LPM, the ULIP challenges students to take responsibility for their work and service, engage with supervisors and coworkers to learn collaboratively, and reflect seriously on their values, beliefs, and vocational goals. Program assessment revealed that experiential learning, partnerships with supervisors, autonomy in work, dissonance, and reflection combined to help interns develop increasingly complex views of themselves as citizens and their role in the larger world (Egart and Healy, 2004).

Innovations in Academic Advising. Academic advising often focuses on helping students make good academic decisions; learning goals such as critical thinking, internally defined values, and responsible citizenship are inherent in these decisions. An academic advising program for students in academic difficulty at a large research university integrates these goals by focusing on effective learning strategies, complex ways of knowing, and students' taking charge of their own lives through developing their goals and values. The structure of the program is designed with the LPM. All one-on-one sessions are conducted as conversations in which the advisor raises questions about students' interests, strengths, goals, motivation level, obstacles to reaching goals, and opinions about how these all relate. Mutual conversation that validates students' perspectives and challenges them to choose paths to resolve issues helps them take responsibility for their academic progress. Studying a diverse group of students who participated in the program for a semester, Pizzolato (2006) reported that participants exhibited greater gains in semester grade point average (53 percent compared to non-program students 28 percent), greater gains in cumulative grade point average (3 percent compared to 2 percent), and less attrition (16 percent versus 34 percent). Although participants did not fully achieve self-authorship, increasing complexity in how they viewed knowledge, their own role in decisions, and how to consider others' wishes contributed to their academic progress. Pizzolato and her research partners began implementing this program in fall 2006 on a larger scale with first-year students in academic difficulty in a TRIO program at another large research university. The history of TRIO is progressive. It began with Upward Bound, which emerged out of the Economic Opportunity Act of 1964 in response to the administration's War on Poverty. In 1965, Talent Search, the second outreach program, was created as part of the Higher Education Act. In 1968, Student Support Services, which was originally known as Special Services for Disadvantaged Students, was authorized by the Higher Education Amendments and became the third in a series of educational opportunity programs. By the late 1960s, the term *TRIO* was coined to describe these federal programs.

This approach to advising resonates with Laughlin and Creamer's suggestions in Chapter Four regarding career advising. They emphasize the need for advisors to help students focus on the process rather than the outcome of career decision making and specifically assist students in working through multiple and contradictory perspectives. Because the relationship with the authority figure was crucial to women in their study, building a strong yet mutual relationship with advisees may help them face the challenges of considering alternatives and incorporating their own voices in these decisions.

Cocurricular Innovations. Cocurricular settings offer rich contexts in which to promote twenty-first-century learning goals and self-authorship. The Community Standards Model (CSM), created at University of Nevada, Las Vegas, and used in many residential life divisions in the country, uses the LPM to help students create shared agreements about how they will treat one another in their living environment. The learning goals include developing a mature sense of identity and mature interdependent relations with diverse others. Although intellectual complexity is not an explicit goal, encountering dissonance among diverse perspectives and participating in crafting these into agreements promotes intellectual development. Groups of residents use the model to establish initial standards, refine standards and solve problems as they arise, and hold community members accountable for violation of the standards. Staff guide the process, carefully balancing empowering students with helping them shape civil and safe living environments. Two-thirds or more of students participating in CSM reported increased understanding of themselves, increased willingness to state their opinion and stand up for their beliefs, a greater understanding and openness to others, and more comfort in making their own decisions. Although not all students achieved self-authorship, those who did not were making progress toward it (Piper and Buckley, 2004).

Honor councils that adjudicate academic dishonesty cases may be another context for promoting self-authorship. Through observing hearings and interviewing honor council members, Cara Appel-Silbaugh (2006) found themes of self-authorship among these members: using ethics and internal values to guide decisions, considering multiple interpretations of a case, upholding policy and procedure despite seeing its shortcomings, and blending integrity, ethics, and emotional sensitivity in decision making. She suggests using the LPM to help students process cases to achieve self-authorship.

Student affairs divisions are exploring self-authorship as an overarching principle to guide their work. The student affairs division at California State University, Northridge, has been guided by a learning-centered vision since 2003. Situated in the context of an overall institutional focus on learning-centered education (Koester, Hellenbrand, and Piper, 2005), the division has worked to define developmental learning outcomes for their practice in each functional area, devise and implement practice to achieve these learning outcomes, and design assessment plans to assess their effectiveness. These efforts are linked to partners outside student affairs. One example is a joint effort of the Career Center and the College of Science and Mathematics that assists students with career exploration to enhance academic success (Koester, Hellenbrand, and Piper, 2005). The University of Michigan is also exploring self-authorship as a foundation for student affairs practice. A committee that was convened to study student climate began to explore the role of development in intercultural maturity. This evolved into using the LPM assessment steps to explore the degree to which various programmatic efforts connected to students' development. The committee is now advancing self-authorship as a guiding principle for constructing optimal learning environments throughout the student affairs division (L. Landreman, personal communication, Mar. 29, 2006).

Innovations in Graduate Education, Professional Staff, and Faculty Development. For more than a decade, the LPM has served as the guiding philosophy to promote self-authorship in the college student personnel master of science program at Miami University. The LPM shaped the evolution of eight core values for the program: integration of theory, inquiry, and practice; creative controversy; self-authorship; self-reflection; situating learning in learners' experiences; a shared commitment to inclusiveness; constructive collaboration; and offering adequate challenge and significant support. These values permeate the curriculum, pedagogy, and community-building efforts of the program. Students consistently report learning a great deal about themselves, collaborating effectively with others, learning to critically analyze multiple perspectives, and self-authoring their own professional beliefs. Faculty also report continuing learning from their mutual partnerships with students (Rogers, Magolda, Baxter Magolda, and Knight-Abowitz, 2004).

The higher education and student affairs graduate program at The Ohio State University is also using LPM as its design philosophy to promote students' intellectual, professional, and personal growth. One of its six professional competency categories includes goals that resonate with twenty-first-century learning outcomes such as critical thinking and problem solving, lifelong learning, ethics, and diversity and multiculturalism. They plan to use the LPM assumptions and principles to design and implement instructional plans (Brischke, Hollingsworth, Shilling, and Welkener, 2006).

Use of the LPM for professional student affairs staff development aided the University of Nevada, Las Vegas, in a structural reorganization also designed with the LPM. Reorienting the student affairs organization to promote student learning and using organizational change models to work toward collaborative leadership, the organization's leaders recognized that promoting self-authorship among the staff was crucial. The complexity of shared leadership required that staff develop self-authorship. The LPM guided their explorations of how they constructed themselves and their social relations, as well as how they viewed new ways of doing their work. Sustained work over a year's time enabled the staff to develop mature working relationships in which they negotiated expectations, reflected on values, and forged partnerships. This enabled the division to translate the LPM to working with students to promote their self-authorship (Mills and Strong, 2004).

Just as a new model of practice required self-authorship on the part of professional staff at the university, incorporating student development and the goal of self-authorship in teaching requires self-authorship on the part of faculty. In Chapter Two of this volume, Terry Wildman emphasized that the shape and pace of students' development is dependent on the shape and pace of educators' development. As he noted, the Center for Excellence in Undergraduate Teaching at Virginia Tech has been engaging faculty in dialogue about the role of student development for ten years. The Earth Sustainability course described in Chapter Five is just one of many innovations that emerged from that conversation. Other innovations that emerged, many of which use the LPM as a framework, include a residential leadership community, faculty dialogues about the scholarship of teaching, use of the constructive-developmental framework in teaching and research (see Laughlin and Creamer's study in Chapter Four), and reconceptualization of a core curriculum (Wildman, 2004).

In Chapter Two in this volume, Wildman advances a new model of faculty development, one that addresses the need to counteract a deeply embedded image of teaching and learning that is inconsistent with promoting self-authorship. It is important to recognize that his proposal of assistive dialogue implements the LPM with the aim of faculty self-authoring their own images of teaching and learning. Placing faculty development in real classrooms situates learning in learners' (in this case, faculty) experience. Exploring ways of teaching and conceptions of learning in this process validates learners as knowers, joins novice and mentor faculty in mutual knowledge construction, and portrays teaching as a complex art form to which one must bring oneself.

In some cases, faculty are predisposed to teach toward self-authorship. Barbara Hooper's work (2006) on the role of faculty members' professional histories revealed that occupational therapy faculty members who had witnessed the importance of self-authorship in their profession brought that vision to their teaching. In these cases, Wildman's advocacy of institutional accommodations to support this kind of teaching is crucial.

Research to Refine Linkages Between Self-Authorship and Learning Outcomes

Despite exciting progress in promoting self-authorship and key learning outcomes across a range of diverse curricular and cocurricular contexts, research to refine linkages between self-authorship and learning outcomes, assessment of self-authorship and learning outcomes, and how self-authorship evolves holistically over time is crucial. Contemporary work in all three categories is underway.

Self-Authorship and Learning Outcomes. The Wabash National Study of Liberal Arts Education is a longitudinal, multi-institution study to explore the institutional conditions, practices, programs, and structures that foster the development and integration of the seven learning outcomes necessary for wise citizenship: the inclination to inquire and life-long learning; leadership; well-being; moral reasoning and character; the integration of learning; effective reasoning and problem solving; and intercultural effectiveness. In-depth interviews conducted on multiple campuses explore students' entering personal characteristics and perspectives, the nature of college experiences students identify as important, how students' initial perspectives and ways of engaging in these experiences combine to help them make sense of their experiences, and how their interpretation of their experiences reflects growth on the seven learning outcomes and the underlying cognitive, intrapersonal, and interpersonal dimensions of self-authorship. This study, launched in fall 2006, will provide insights about the relationship between learning outcomes and self-authorship, as well as the educational practices that promote both.

Assessing Self-Authorship and Learning Outcomes. As Barbara Bekken and Joan Marie reported in Chapter Five, they are assessing progress on both learning outcomes (critical thinking, scientific reasoning, and student engagement) and self-authorship in the Earth Sustainability course series. Their work demonstrates that course assignments used to promote learning can also be used to assess progress on learning outcomes. Engaging students in reflecting on their previous work near the end of the semester also serves to assess developmental progress. In addition to the assessment reported in Chapter Five, they are assessing self-authorship through the use of the measure of epistemological reflection (Baxter Magolda, 2001a), a short essay questionnaire to measure intellectual development, Pizzolato's self-authorship survey described in Chapter Three, and in-depth interviews. Their plan to follow participants in Earth Sustainability as well as control group participants longitudinally will provide insights into how an intentionally developmental curriculum and learning partnerships pedagogy promote critical thinking, scientific reasoning, and self-authorship.

The Earth Sustainability series assessment plan also holds promise for clarifying important issues in assessing self-authorship. As Pizzolato notes in Chapter Three, assessing self-authorship is a complex challenge. The questions she raises regarding the combination of reasoning and action in determining self-authorship exacerbate the difficulty in understanding how students view knowledge, themselves, and their relationships. Recognition instruments that accurately assess development have been difficult to create because students often prefer language more complex than what they can freely produce (Baxter Magolda and Porterfield, 1988; Gibbs and Widaman, 1982). Pizzolato's points about how students interpret the language on a questionnaire also complicate educators' ability to acquire a clear picture of students' development. Laughlin and Creamer's commentary in Chapter Four on the nuances they discovered using mixed methods suggests that their interview data offered a window into how students constructed their consultations with others on career decisions that was not evident in their reports of whom they consulted on the questionnaire. Many assessment researchers argue that naturalistic methods best capture self-authorship (Baxter Magolda, 2001a; Wood, Kitchener, and Jensen, 2002). That said, Pizzolato's continued work on the self-authorship survey is crucial to determining whether recognition instruments can be constructed to assess the complexity of self-authorship, as are mixed-method explorations.

A combination of course assignments, student reflections, educator analysis of student work, and in-depth interviews are the means to assess both learning outcomes and self-authorship. Haynes's revision of the Honors and Scholars program, Yonkers-Talz's ongoing longitudinal study of Casa participants, and Bekken and Marie's longitudinal assessment of Earth Sustainability participants all use this combination.

Longitudinal Studies. In addition to the projects described, longitudinal studies of young adult populations' development continue to refine our understanding of the evolution and integration of multiple dimensions of self-authorship. Vasti Torres's multi-institutional study of Latino and Latina college students (Torres, 2003; Torres and Baxter Magolda, 2004) reveals the intersections of familial relationships, cognitive dissonance, and ethnic identity development in the journey toward self-authorship. Elisa Abes's study of lesbian college students informs the complex dynamics of sexual orientation in the evolution of cognitive, identity, and relationship growth (Abes, 2003; Abes and Jones, 2004). My longitudinal study, which began with college student participants who are now approaching age forty, provides a window into how cognitive, intrapersonal, and interpersonal dimensions of development intertwine as adults engage in the complexity of professional, public, and personal life in the twenty-first century.

The Promise of Self-Authorship

As Terry Wildman articulated in Chapter Two, helping students achieve twenty-first-century learning outcomes and advanced intellectual growth requires bringing together what we know about learning, development, instruction, and assessment to shape educational practice. This volume highlights what we currently know and ongoing inquiry into all four of these arenas and how they can be intentionally combined to form effective educational practice. Wildman's point about educators' transforming their conceptualizations of learning, development, instruction, and assessment is particularly important. Our understanding of how self-authorship and learning evolve, as well as the necessity of self-authorship for success in college and adult life, makes it imperative for educators to shift from old, controlling designs to new partnership designs. We hope the theoretical and assessment advances and tangible examples of successful innovative practice throughout this volume provide educators the knowledge and motivation to reenvision their educational practice.

References

Abes, E. S. "The Dynamics of Lesbian College Students' Multiple Dimensions of Identity." Unpublished doctoral dissertation, Ohio State University, 2003.

Abes, E. S., and Jones, S. R. "Meaning-Making Capacity and the Dynamics of Lesbian College Students' Multiple Dimensions of Identity." *Journal of College Student Development*, 2004, *45*(6), 612–632.

Appel-Silbaugh, C. "Acting Out Integrity: Student Honor Council Members and Self-Authorship." Paper presented at the American College Personnel Association, Indianapolis, Ind., Mar. 2006.

Baxter Magolda, M. B. "A Constructivist Revision of the Measure of Epistemological Reflection." *Journal of College Student Development*, 2001a, *42*(6), 520–534.

Baxter Magolda, M. B. *Making Their Own Way: Narratives for Transforming Higher Education to Promote Self-Development.* Sterling, Va.: Stylus, 2001b.

Baxter Magolda, M. B. "Learning Partnerships Model: A Framework for Promoting Self-Authorship." In M. B. Baxter Magolda and P. M. King (eds.), *Learning Partnerships: Theory and Models of Practice to Educate for Self-Authorship.* Sterling, Va.: Stylus, 2004a.

Baxter Magolda, M. B. "Self-Authorship as the Common Goal of 21st Century Education." In M. B. Baxter Magolda and P. M. King (eds.), *Learning Partnerships: Theory and Models of Practice to Educate for Self-Authorship.* Sterling, Va.: Stylus, 2004b.

Baxter Magolda, M. B., and Porterfield, W. D. *Assessing Intellectual Development: The Link Between Theory and Practice.* Alexandria, Va.: American College Personnel Association, 1988.

Brischke, K., Hollingsworth, R., Shilling, S., and Welkener, M. "Making a Difference in the Professional Development of Graduate Students." Paper presented at the American College Personnel Association, Indianapolis, Ind., Mar. 2006.

Egart, K., and Healy, M. "An Urban Leadership Internship Program: Implementing Learning Partnerships 'Unplugged' from Campus Structures." In M. B. Baxter Magolda and P. M. King (eds.), *Learning Partnerships: Theory and Models of Practice to Educate for Self-Authorship.* Sterling, Va.: Stylus, 2004.

Gibbs, J., and Widaman, K. F. *Social Intelligence: Measuring the Development of Sociomoral Reflection.* Upper Saddle River, N.J.: Prentice Hall, 1982.

Haynes, C. "Promoting Self-Authorship Through an Interdisciplinary Writing Curriculum." In M. B. Baxter Magolda and P. M. King (eds.), *Learning Partnerships: Theory and Models of Practice to Educate for Self-Authorship.* Sterling, Va.: Stylus, 2004.

Haynes, C. "The Integrated Student: Fostering Holistic Development to Enhance Learning." *About Campus: Enriching the Student Learning Experience,* 2006, *10*(6), 17–23.

Helsing, D., Broderick, M., and Hammerman, J. "A Developmental View of ESOL Students' Identity Transitions in an Urban Community College." In R. Kegan (ed.), *Toward a New Pluralism in ABE/EDOL Classrooms: Teaching to Multiple "Cultures of Mind."* Cambridge, Mass.: National Center for the Study of Adult Learning and Literacy, Harvard Graduate School of Education, 2001.

Hooper, B. "Teaching for Self-Authorship in Graduate Professional Education: The Role of Faculty Biography." Unpublished manuscript, 2006.

Hornak, A., and Ortiz, A. M. "Creating a Context to Promote Diversity Education and Self-Authorship Among Community College Students." In M. B. Baxter Magolda and P. M. King (eds.), *Learning Partnerships: Theory and Models of Practice to Educate for Self-Authorship.* Sterling, Va.: Stylus, 2004.

Kegan, R. *In over Our Heads: The Mental Demands of Modern Life.* Cambridge, Mass.: Harvard University Press, 1994.

King, P. M., and Baxter Magolda, M. B. "A Developmental Model of Intercultural Maturity." *Journal of College Student Development,* 2005, *46*(6), 571–592.

Koester, J., Hellenbrand, H., and Piper, T. D. "Exploring the Actions Behind the Words 'Learning-Centered Institution.'" *About Campus: Enriching the Student Learning Experience,* 2005, *10*(4), 10–16.

Mezirow, J. (ed.). *Learning as Transformation: Critical Perspectives on a Theory in Progress.* San Francisco: Jossey-Bass, 2000.

Mills, R., and Strong, K. L. "Organizing for Learning in a Division of Student Affairs." In M. B. Baxter Magolda and P. M. King (eds.), *Learning Partnerships: Theory and Models of Practice to Educate for Self-Authorship.* Sterling, Va.: Stylus, 2004.

Piper, T. D., and Buckley, J. A. "Community Standards Model: Developing Learning Partnerships in Campus Housing." In M. B. Baxter Magolda and P. M. King (eds.), *Learning Partnerships: Theory and Models of Practice to Educate for Self-Authorship.* Sterling, Va.: Stylus, 2004.

Pizzolato, J. E. "Developing Self-Authorship: Exploring the Experiences of High-Risk College Students." *Journal of College Student Development,* 2003, *44*(6), 797–812.

Pizzolato, J. E. "Coping with Conflict: Self-Authorship, Coping, and Adaptation to College in First-Year, High-Risk Students." *Journal of College Student Development,* 2004, *45*(4), 425–442.

Pizzolato, J. E. "Creating Crossroads for Self-Authorship: Investigating the Provocative Moment." *Journal of College Student Development,* 2005, *46*(6), 624–641.

Pizzolato, J. "Implementing Learning Partnerships, Assessing Self-Authorship: Implications from a Case Study." Paper presented at the American College Personnel Association, Indianapolis, Ind., Mar. 2006.

Rogers, J. L., Magolda, P. M., Baxter Magolda, M. B., and Knight-Abowitz, K. "A Community of Scholars: Enacting the Learning Partnerships Model in Graduate Education." In M. B. Baxter Magolda and P. M. King (eds.), *Learning Partnerships: Theory and Models of Practice to Educate for Self-Authorship.* Sterling, Va.: Stylus, 2004.

Torres, V. "Factors Influencing Ethnic Identity Development of Latino College Students in the First Two Years of College." *Journal of College Student Development,* 2003, *44*(4), 532–547.

Torres, V., and Baxter Magolda, M. B. "Reconstructing Latino Identity: The Influence of Cognitive Development on the Ethnic Identity Process of Latino Students." *Journal of College Student Development,* 2004, *45*(3), 333–347.

Wildman, T. M. "The Learning Partnerships Model: Framing Faculty and Institutional Development." In M. B. Baxter Magolda and P. M. King (eds.), *Learning Partnerships: Theory and Models of Practice to Educate for Self-Authorship.* Sterling, Va.: Stylus, 2004.

Wood, P., Kitchener, K. S., and Jensen, L. "Considerations in the Design and Evaluation of a Paper-and-Pencil Measure of Epistemic Cognition." In B. K. Hofer and P. R. Pintrich (eds.), *Personal Epistemology: The Psychology of Beliefs About Knowledge and Knowing.* Mahwah, N.J.: Erlbaum, 2002.

Yonkers-Talz, K. "A Learning Partnership: U.S. College Students and the Poor in El Salvador." In M. B. Baxter Magolda and P. M. King (eds.), *Learning Partnerships: Theory and Models of Practice to Educate for Self-Authorship.* Sterling, Va.: Stylus, 2004.

MARCIA B. BAXTER MAGOLDA is Distinguished Professor of Educational Leadership at Miami University, Ohio.

7

This chapter reiterates the need for attention to the journey of self-authorship and suggests next steps for institutions and educators.

The Journey of Self-Authorship: Next Steps to the Destination

Peggy S. Meszaros

This volume of *New Directions for Teaching and Learning* has focused on bringing the new lens of self-authorship to guide the intellectual growth of college students. Accountability efforts underway seem headed to national testing of narrow subject matter knowledge that may negate the broader goals of student intellectual development. This volume has made the case for institutional and faculty changes needed to broaden thinking about student learning goals and outcomes within the framework of the theory of self-authorship and the Learning Partnerships Model (LPM), a model of support and guidance that links learning and development. There are four action steps to broaden the discussion and provide faculty and student affairs professionals with the tools they need to advance the intellectual development of their students:

1. Read and reflect on this volume; then share it with colleagues who are concerned and engaged with student development in its broadest sense. You might host a discussion group of faculty and student affairs professionals to delve into the ideas and examples provided throughout the volume and make plans for your work together. You would be bringing together two worlds, academe and student affairs, that do not usually sit together to talk about their mutual student concerns. You may also spur some thinking about projects you could undertake related to some of the ideas and examples in the volume.

2. Make an appointment with your department head, dean, supervisor, provost, or whomever you report to and share the volume with this person, paying special attention to Chapter Two on needed institutional changes to

NEW DIRECTIONS FOR TEACHING AND LEARNING, no. 109, Spring 2007 © Wiley Periodicals, Inc.
Published online in Wiley InterScience (www.interscience.wiley.com) • DOI: 10.1002/tl.267

break the old paradigms. Plan with this administrator ways you and she or he can help move the dialogue along with other administrators so that you build a support group of colleagues at your institution who are deeply involved with advancing the intellectual growth of students.

3. Continue to read widely to update yourself on the outcomes of national groups like the Commission on the Future of Higher Education and other reports mentioned in Chapter One. This reading will help you fashion responses such as rethinking student learning outcomes for your program or LPM demonstration projects in research or curricular developments for your campus. This continued reading will keep you thinking about using the lens of self-authorship in new ways for the benefit of students.

4. Look for new resources to help faculty and student affairs profession-als do their job of fostering student intellectual growth, whether in the class-room, advising, or some other campus setting. One new practical resource that uses the theory base of self-authorship was developed by Meszaros and Laugh-lin (2006; found at http://www.witvideo.org.vt.edu). At this site, you will find information about a DVD and the facilitator's guide, *The Power of Partners: Helping Girls Find Their Way to High Tech Careers,* produced from research funded by the National Science Foundation. You can see a clip of the DVD and order the materials directly from the site. The facilitator's guide has sessions for parents, college advisors, school counselors, and teachers and offers advice and insights on using the theory of self-authorship and the LPM for these groups of educators and supporters. Originally developed to focus on informa-tion technology career choices and females, the information is equally applic-able for boys and can be extended to all science, technology, engineering, and math fields. The advice and support for educators working with college stu-dents in career decision making builds on developing self-authorship. The metaphor for the LPM used in Chapter One—of the tandem bike—is used throughout to explain the challenge and support tenets of self-authorship.

These four action steps are a starting point. I am sure that you will think of other steps to take as you begin your own personal journey to learn more about advancing the intellectual growth of students. The destination we all seek is a sound approach, built on a solid theoretical foundation and a model for teaching and learning, that will advance the intellectual growth of college students.

Reference

Meszaros, P., and Laughlin, A. *The Power of Partners: Helping Females Find Their Way to High Tech Careers.* Washington, D.C.: National Science Foundation, 2006. DVD.

PEGGY S. MESZAROS *is the William E. Lavery Professor of Human Development and director of the Center for Information Technology Impacts on Children, Youth, and Families at Virginia Polytechnic Institute and State University in Blacksburg, Virginia.*

INDEX

NEW DIRECTIONS FOR TEACHING AND LEARNING
Order Form
SUBSCRIPTIONS AND SINGLE ISSUES

Use this form to receive **20% off** all back issues of New Directions for Teaching and Learning. All single issues priced at **$23.20** (normally $29.00)

TITLE	ISSUE NO.	ISBN
_____	_____	_____
_____	_____	_____
_____	_____	_____

Call 888-378-2537 or see mailing instructions below. When calling, mention the promotional code, JB7ND, to receive your discount.

SUBSCRIPTIONS: (1 year, 4 issues)

☐ New Order   ☐ Renewal

U.S.	☐ Individual: $80	☐ Institutional: $195
Canada/Mexico	☐ Individual: $80	☐ Institutional: $235
All Others	☐ Individual: $104	☐ Institutional: $269

Call 888-378-2537 or see mailing and pricing instructions below. Online subscriptions are available at www.interscience.wiley.com.

Copy or detach page and send to:
John Wiley & Sons, Journals Dept, 5th Floor
989 Market Street, San Francisco, CA 94103-1741
Order Form can also be faxed to: 888-481-2665

Issue/Subscription Amount: $ _____	**SHIPPING CHARGES:**
Shipping Amount: $ _____	SURFACE Dometic Canadian
(for single issues only—subscription prices include shipping)	First Item $5.00 $6.00
Total Amount: $ _____	Each Add'l Item $3.00 $1.50

(No sales tax for U.S. subscriptions. Canadian residents, add GST for subscription orders. Individual rate subscriptions must be paid by personal check or credit card. Individual rate subscriptions may not be resold as library copies.)

☐ Payment enclosed (U.S. check or money order only. All payments must be in U.S. dollars.)

☐ VISA ☐ MC ☐ Amex # _____ Exp. Date _____

Card Holder Name _____ Card Issue # _____

Signature_____ Day Phone _____

☐ Bill Me (U.S. institutional orders only. Purchase order required.)

Purchase order # _____
Federal Tax ID13559302   GST 89102 8052

Name_____

Address _____

Phone _____ E-mail _____

spirituality is viewed, taught, and experienced is intensely personal. The goal is not to prescribe a method for integrating spirituality but to offer options and perspectives. Readers will be reminded that the quest for truth and meaning, not the destination, is what is vitally important.
ISBN: 0-7879-8363-2

TL103   Identity, Learning, and the Liberal Arts
Ned Scott Laff
Argues that we must foster conversations between liberal studies and student development theory, because the skills inherent in liberal learning are the same skills used for personal development. Students need to experience core learning that truly influences their critical thinking skills, character development, and ethics. Educators need to design student learning encounters that develop these areas. This volume gives examples of how liberal arts education can be a healthy foundation for life skills.
ISBN: 0-7879-8333-0

TL102   Advancing Faculty Learning Through Interdisciplinary Collaboration
Elizabeth G. Creamer, Lisa R. Lattuca
Explores why stakeholders in higher education should refocus attention on collaboration as a form of faculty learning. Chapters give theoretical basis then practical case studies for collaboration's benefits in outreach, scholarship, and teaching. Also discusses impacts on education policy, faculty hiring and development, and assessment of collaborative work.
ISBN: 0-7879-8070-6

TL101   Enhancing Learning with Laptops in the Classroom
Linda B. Nilson, Barbara E. Weaver
This volume contains case studies—mostly from Clemson University's leading-edge laptop program—that address victories as well as glitches in teaching with laptop computers in the classroom. Disciplines using laptops include psychology, music, statistics, animal sciences, and humanities. The volume also advises faculty on making a laptop mandate successful at their university, with practical guidance for both pedagogy and student learning.
ISBN: 0-7879-8049-8

TL100   Alternative Strategies for Evaluating Student Learning
Michelle V. Achacoso, Marilla D. Svinicki
Teaching methods are adapting to the modern era, but innovation in assessment of student learning lags behind. This volume examines theory and practical examples of creative new methods of evaluation, including authentic testing, testing with multimedia, portfolios, group exams, visual synthesis, and performance-based testing. Also investigates improving students' ability to take and learn from tests, before and after.
ISBN: 0-7879-7970-8

TL99   Addressing Faculty and Student Classroom Improprieties
John M. Braxton, Alan E. Bayer
Covers the results of a large research study on occurrence and perceptions of classroom improprieties by both students and faculty. When classroom norms are violated, all parties in a classroom are affected, and teaching and learning suffer. The authors offer guidelines for both student and faculty classroom behavior and how institutions might implement those suggestions.
ISBN: 0-7879-7794-2

TL98   Decoding the Disciplines: Helping Students Learn Disciplinary Ways of Thinking
David Pace, Joan Middendorf
The Decoding the Disciplines model is a way to teach students the critical-thinking skills required to understand their specific discipline. Faculty define bottlenecks to learning, dissect the ways experts deal with the problematic issues, and invent ways to model experts' thinking for students. Chapters are written by faculty in diverse fields who successfully used these methods and became involved in the scholarship of teaching and learning.
ISBN: 0-7879-7789-6

TL97   Building Faculty Learning Communities
Milton D. Cox, Laurie Richlin
A very effective way to address institutional challenges is a faculty learning community. FLCs are useful for preparing future faculty, reinvigorating senior faculty, and implementing new courses, curricula, or campus initiatives. The results of FLCs parallel those of student learning communities, such as retention, deeper learning, respect for others, and greater civic participation. This volume describes FLCs from a practitioner's perspective, with plenty of advice, wisdom, and lessons for starting your own FLC.
ISBN: 0-7879-7568-0

TL96   Online Student Ratings of Instruction
Trav D. Johnson, D. Lynn Sorenson
Many institutions are adopting Web-based student ratings of instruction, or are considering doing it, because online systems have the potential to save time and money among other benefits. But they also present a number of challenges. The authors of this volume have firsthand experience with electronic ratings of instruction. They identify the advantages, consider costs and benefits, explain their solutions, and provide recommendations on how to facilitate online ratings.
ISBN: 0-7879-7262-2

TL95   Problem-Based Learning in the Information Age
Dave S. Knowlton, David C. Sharp
Provides information about theories and practices associated with problem-based learning, a pedagogy that allows students to become more engaged in their own education by actively interpreting information. Today's professors are adopting problem-based learning across all disciplines to facilate a broader, modern definition of what it means to learn. Authors provide practical experience about designing useful problems, creating conducive learning environments, facilitating students' activities, and assessing students' efforts at problem solving.
ISBN: 0-7879-7172-3

TL94   Technology: Taking the Distance out of Learning
Margit Misangyi Watts
This volume addresses the possibilities and challenges of computer technology in higher education. The contributors examine the pressures to use technology, the reasons not to, the benefits of it, the feeling of being a learner as well as a teacher, the role of distance education, and the place of computers in the modern world. Rather than discussing only specific successes or failures, this issue addresses computers as a new cultural

symbol and begins meaningful conversations about technology in general and how it affects education in particular.
ISBN: 0-7879-6989-3

TL93   Valuing and Supporting Undergraduate Research
Joyce Kinkead
The authors gathered in this volume share a deep belief in the value of undergraduate research. Research helps students develop skills in problem solving, critical thinking, and communication, and undergraduate researchers' work can contribute to an institution's quest to further knowledge and help meet societal challenges. Chapters provide an overview of undergraduate research, explore programs at different types of institutions, and offer suggestions on how faculty members can find ways to work with undergraduate researchers.
ISBN: 0-7879-6907-9

TL92   The Importance of Physical Space in Creating Supportive Learning Environments
Nancy Van Note Chism, Deborah J. Bickford
The lack of extensive dialogue on the importance of learning spaces in higher education environments prompted the essays in this volume. Chapter authors look at the topic of learning spaces from a variety of perspectives, elaborating on the relationship between physical space and learning, arguing for an expanded notion of the concept of learning spaces and furnishings, talking about the context within which decision making for learning spaces takes place, and discussing promising approaches to the renovation of old learning spaces and the construction of new ones.
ISBN: 0-7879-6344-5

TL91   Assessment Strategies for the On-Line Class: From Theory to Practice
Rebecca S. Anderson, John F. Bauer, Bruce W. Speck
Addresses the kinds of questions that instructors need to ask themselves as they begin to move at least part of their students' work to an on-line format. Presents an initial overview of the need for evaluating students' on-line work with the same care that instructors give to the work in hard-copy format. Helps guide instructors who are considering using on-line learning in conjunction with their regular classes, as well as those interested in going totally on-line.
ISBN: 0-7879-6343-7

TL90   Scholarship in the Postmodern Era: New Venues, New Values, New Visions
Kenneth J. Zahorski
A little over a decade ago, Ernest Boyer's *Scholarship Reconsidered* burst upon the academic scene, igniting a robust national conversation that maintains its vitality to this day. This volume aims at advancing that important conversation. Its first section focuses on the new settings and circumstances in which the act of scholarship is being played out; its second identifies and explores the fresh set of values currently informing today's scholarly practices; and its third looks to the future of scholarship, identifying trends, causative factors, and potentialities that promise to shape scholars and their scholarship in the new millennium.
ISBN: 0-7879-6293-7

TL89   Applying the Science of Learning to University Teaching and Beyond
        Diane F. Halpern, Milton D. Hakel
        Seeks to build on empirically validated learning activities to enhance what and
        how much is learned and how well and how long it is remembered. Demon-
        strates that the movement for a real science of learning—the application of
        scientific principles to the study of learning—has taken hold both under the
        controlled conditions of the laboratory and in the messy real-world settings
        where most of us go about the business of teaching and learning.
        ISBN: 0-7879-5791-7

TL88   Fresh Approaches to the Evaluation of Teaching
        Christopher Knapper, Patricia Cranton
        Describes a number of alternative approaches, including interpretive and
        critical evaluation, use of teaching portfolios and teaching awards,
        performance indicators and learning outcomes, technology-mediated
        evaluation systems, and the role of teacher accreditation and teaching
        scholarship in instructional evaluation.
        ISBN: 0-7879-5789-5

TL87   Techniques and Strategies for Interpreting Student Evaluations
        Karron G. Lewis
        Focuses on all phases of the student rating process—from data-gathering
        methods to presentation of results. Topics include methods of encouraging
        meaningful evaluations, mid-semester feedback, uses of quality teams and
        focus groups, and creating questions that target individual faculty needs and
        interest.
        ISBN: 0-7879-5789-5

TL86   Scholarship Revisited: Perspectives on the Scholarship of Teaching
        Carolin Kreber
        Presents the outcomes of a Delphi Study conducted by an international
        panel of academics working in faculty evaluation scholarship and
        postsecondary teaching and learning. Identifies the important components of
        scholarship of teaching, defines its characteristics and outcomes, and
        explores its most pressing issues.
        ISBN: 0-7879-5447-0

TL85   Beyond Teaching to Mentoring
        Alice G. Reinarz, Eric R. White
        Offers guidelines to optimizing student learning through classroom activities
        as well as peer, faculty, and professional mentoring. Addresses mentoring
        techniques in technical training, undergraduate business, science, and liberal
        arts studies, health professions, international study, and interdisciplinary
        work.
        ISBN: 0-7879-5617-1

TL84   Principles of Effective Teaching in the Online Classroom
        Renée E. Weiss, Dave S. Knowlton, Bruce W. Speck
        Discusses structuring the online course, utilizing resources from the World
        Wide Web and using other electronic tools and technology to enhance
        classroom efficiency. Addresses challenges unique to the online classroom
        community, including successful communication strategies, performance
        evaluation, academic integrity, and accessibility for disabled students.
        ISBN: 0-7879-5615-5

NEW DIRECTIONS FOR TEACHING AND LEARNING IS NOW AVAILABLE ONLINE AT WILEY INTERSCIENCE

What is Wiley InterScience?

Wiley InterScience is the dynamic online content service from John Wiley & Sons delivering the full text of over 300 leading scientific, technical, medical, and professional journals, plus major reference works, the acclaimed Current Protocols laboratory manuals, and even the full text of select Wiley print books online.

What are some special features of Wiley InterScience?

Wiley Interscience Alerts is a service that delivers table of contents via e-mail for any journal available on Wiley InterScience as soon as a new issue is published online.
EarlyView is Wiley's exclusive service presenting individual articles online as soon as they are ready, even before the release of the compiled print issue. These articles are complete, peer-reviewed, and citable.
CrossRef is the innovative multi-publisher reference linking system enabling readers to move seamlessly from a reference in a journal article to the cited publication, typically located on a different server and published by a different publisher.

How can I access Wiley InterScience?

Visit http://www.interscience.wiley.com.

Guest Users can browse Wiley InterScience for unrestricted access to journal tables of contents and article abstracts, or use the powerful search engine.
Registered Users are provided with a *Personal Home Page* to store and manage customized alerts, searches, and links to favorite journals and articles. Additionally, Registered Users can view free online sample issues and preview selected material from major reference works.
Licensed Customers are entitled to access full-text journal articles in PDF, with select journals also offering full-text HTML.

How do I become an Authorized User?

Authorized Users are individuals authorized by a paying Customer to have access to the journals in Wiley InterScience. For example, a university that subscribes to Wiley journals is considered to be the Customer.
Faculty, staff and students authorized by the university to have access to those journals in Wiley InterScience are Authorized Users. Users should contact their library for information on which Wiley journals they have access to in Wiley InterScience.

ASK YOUR INSTITUTION ABOUT WILEY INTERSCIENCE TODAY!